Yo
2004 POETR

ONCE UPON A RHYME

IMAGINATION FOR
A NEW GENERATION

North West England
Edited by Steve Twelvetree

 Young**Writers**

First published in Great Britain in 2004 by:
Young Writers
Remus House
Coltsfoot Drive
Peterborough
PE2 9JX
Telephone: 01733 890066
Website: www.youngwriters.co.uk

SB ISBN 1 84460 425 X

Foreword

Young Writers was established in 1991 and has been passionately devoted to the promotion of reading and writing in children and young adults ever since. The quest continues today. Young Writers remains as committed to engendering the fostering of burgeoning poetic and literary talent as ever.

This year's Young Writers competition has proven as vibrant and dynamic as ever and we are delighted to present a showcase of the best poetry from across the UK. Each poem has been carefully selected from a wealth of *Once Upon A Rhyme* entries before ultimately being published in this, our twelfth primary school poetry series.

Once again, we have been supremely impressed by the overall high quality of the entries we have received. The imagination, energy and creativity which has gone into each young writer's entry made choosing the best poems a challenging and often difficult but ultimately hugely rewarding task - the general high standard of the work submitted amply vindicating this opportunity to bring their poetry to a larger appreciative audience.

We sincerely hope you are pleased with our final selection and that you will enjoy *Once Upon A Rhyme North West England* for many years to come.

Contents

Guy Runnels-Moss (10)	16
Katharine McCormack (10)	17
Pippa Christian (11)	17
Charlotte Thornton (10)	18
David Bond (11)	18
Philip Kelly (11)	19
Georgia Morgan (10)	19
Fiona Boardman (11)	20
Holly Mills (11)	20
Rachael McKeown (10)	21
Bethany Leader (10)	22
Joseph Walsh (11)	23
Rachel Wignall (10)	23
Francesca Wai (11)	24
Rachel Kelly (11)	24

Brennands Endowed Primary School, Slaidburn

James Harrison (9)	25
Mick Handley (9)	25
Jordan Gott (9)	26
David Robinson (10)	26
Alexandra Riley (7)	26
Daniel Parker (11)	27
Sarah Tedstone (9)	27
Seth Blakey (10)	28
Alice Waddington (9)	28
Anna Blakey (7)	29
Michael Roberts (10)	29
Jessica Fogie (8)	30

Brindle St James CE Primary School, Brindle

Max Harwood (8)	30
Rebecca Baines (8)	31
Benjamin Nuttall (8)	31
Megan Jenkinson (8)	32
Jake Davenport (7)	32
James Gregory (9)	33
Penny Woodhouse (8)	33

Constable Lee St Paul's CE Primary School, Rossendale

Luke Norman (11)	34
Becci Waterhouse (11)	35
Natasha Gregory	35
Adam Smith (11)	36
Lucie Greenwood (11)	37
Ashleigh Colquhoun (10)	38
Jessica Ainsworth (11)	39
Alex Stokes (9)	40
Bethany Holt (10)	41
Lewis Taylor (11)	41
Alaina Homer (10)	42
Anna Shahid (10)	43
Rebecca Ashworth (10)	44
Luke Mason (10)	45
Emma Lancaster (10)	45
Sarah Durham (10)	46
Andrew Allcock (11)	47
David Adams (11)	48
Catherine Hasleden (9)	49
Jeni Greenwood (11)	50

Didsbury Road Primary School, Stockport

Ali Asghar Mahmood (11)	51
Stephen Shackleton (11)	51
James McCalla (11)	52
Jack Oswald (10)	52
Olivia Cork (10)	53
Ali Keshani (11)	53
Katy Stonehouse (10)	54
Georgina Pedler (11)	54
Ryan Williams (10)	55
Daniel Quinn (10)	55
Megan Hughes (11)	56
Aisha Mahmood (11)	56
James Connor (10)	57
Philip Kemp (10)	57
Stephanie Foster (10)	57
Alastair Poole (10)	58
Bardia Nekooie (11)	58
Rashpal Cheema (10)	58

Hasina Sattar (10)	59
Callum Hampson (11)	59
Joe Parker (11)	59
Jack Whitehurst (10)	60
Mike Oates (10)	60
Jamie Webb (10)	61
Matthew Pilling (11)	61
Nicholas Tattersall Baker (11)	62
Jessica Davenport (11)	62
Matthew Ryley (11)	63
Stephen Bailey (10)	63
Jonathan Garner (10)	64
Mosa Jassim (11)	64
Daniel Parsons (10)	65
Elizabeth Powers (10)	65
Sami Haddad (10)	66
Martine Waterhouse (11)	66
Adam Corbridge (11)	67
Salman Ahmed (10)	67
Yan Trinh (11)	68
Dani Cunningham (10)	69
Aisha Yakub (10)	69
Sophia Georgiou (11)	70
Luke Doubleday (10)	70
James Smith (11)	71
Megan Whitehurst (11)	72
Robbie Ford (10)	72
Mai Vi Giang (11)	72
Jack Howden (10)	73

East Crompton St George's CE Primary School, Shaw

Sarah Cole (10)	73
Rebecca Ireland (10)	74
Ellis Bradbury (10)	75
Abigail Rennie (11)	76
Andrew May (10)	77
Jason Slicker (11)	77
Kyle Percy (11)	78

Gregson Lane Primary School, Hoghton

Ammaarah Vorajee (10)	79

Holy Family School, Sale

Holly Davies-Hughes (9)	79
Erin-Kate Bonsall (9)	80
Nathan Percy (9)	80
Dean Giblin (10)	81
Zoe Coombs (8)	81
Rachel Lee (9)	82
Thomas Beveridge (9)	82
Liam Conway (10)	83
Ellen Sara Elizabeth Cagney (9)	83
Ryan Cagney (9)	83

Ightenhill Primary School, Burnley

Alex Berry (9)	84
Shannon Donnelly (8)	84
Thomas Ryland (8)	85
Nathan Tattersall (9)	85
Jamie Catlow (9)	85

Liscard Primary School, Wallasey

Laura Woods (11)	86
Danielle Porter (10)	86
Grace Joy (10)	87
Michaela Johnson (10)	88
Georgia Thompson (10)	89
Jade Wharton (11)	90
Callum Rutherford (10)	91
Sam Shaw (11)	92
Ryan O'Neill (10)	93
Ellen Cooper (10)	93
Rachel Hodgson (11)	94
Liam Roberts (11)	94
Chloe Cunningham (11)	95
John McAfee (11)	96
Danielle Hall (11)	97
Jonathan Addyman (10)	98
Sarah Finnigan (10)	99
Lisa Kinnear (10)	100
Natalie Eastwood (10)	101
Gemma Wright (11)	102
Lewis Simpson (10)	102

Connor Wray (11)	103
Owain Pierce-Hayes (10)	104
James Harrison (11)	105

Lostock Gralam CE Primary School, Northwich

James Hammond (10)	105
Ben Cooper (10)	106
Matthew McKechnie (10)	106
Liz Atherton (10)	107
Donna Edwards (11)	108
Daniel Kenneth Grannell (11)	109
Ryan Whitlow (10)	110
Hannah Thorp (10)	111
Ian Hindmarch (10)	112
Megan Morrell (10)	112
Jonathan Lightfoot (11)	113
Philippa Cavanagh (10)	114
Conor Hardman (10)	115
Bradley Sutton (10)	116
Sam Illidge (11)	117
Ben Dean (10)	118
Daniel Johnson (9)	119
Phillip Clark (11)	120
Jack Canniffe (10)	121
Joanne Cragg (10)	122
Michael Perry (9)	123
Victor Depenha (10)	124
Joel Evans (10)	125

Marsh Green Primary School, Wigan

Christian Richardson (10)	125
John Neville (10)	126
Kieran Dixon (10)	126
Adam Hunter (10)	127
Robyn & John	127
Dionne Forshaw (10)	128
Sarah Louise Dawson (10)	129
Dale	129
Kelly Sharpe (10)	130
Paul Marcroft (10)	130
Leon Speakman (10)	131

Robert Robinson (10)   132
Natalie Riley (10)   133
Andrew James Unsworth (10)   134
Andrew Murray (10)   135
Daryl Ravden (10)   136
Dalton Bleakley (10)   137
Rebecca Browitt (10)   138
Daniel Unsworth (10)   139
Craig Ravden (10)   140
Elizabeth Connolly (10)   141

Marton Primary School, Blackpool
James Brindley (10)   141
Bethany Butler (10)   142
Connor Willoughby (11)   142
Ben Raby (10)   142
Olivia Freitas (11)   143
Ryan Calvert (10)   143
Rebecca Fletcher (10)   143
Ashleigh Alladice (10)   144
Daniel Taylor (11)   144
Sam Purvis (11)   145
Lauren Sarah Sanderson-Roberts (11)   145
Rachel Brown (11)   146
Joshua Alderson (10)   146

Neston Primary School, Little Neston
Steven Barnes-Smith (10)   147
Tom Lancaster (10)   147
Emily Tedford (9)   148
Corrine Abel (10)   148
David Chambers (10)   149
Kyle Griffiths (9)   149
Faye Williams (11)   149
Adam Harbour (10)   150
Daniel Green (9)   150
Dean Jones (11)   150
Jenny Dalziel (9)   151
Jason Brookes (10)   151
Ryan Butterworth (11)   151
Natalie Williams (10)   152

Romiley Primary School, Romiley

Timmy Parker (9)	168
Gemma Lewis (8)	168
Oliver Norman (9)	168
Ella Osiyemi (8)	169
Harley Duffy (8)	169
Jessica Woolridge (9)	169
Eleanor Gilbert (9)	170
Amie Meadows (9)	170
Sam Fazackerley (8)	171
Grace Donovan (8)	171
Ben Jones (9)	172
Eva Morewood (8)	172
James Prike (9)	173
Jasmine Crone (8)	173
Paige Wilkinson (9)	174
Emily Schofield (9)	174
Naomi S Pollitt (8)	175
Morgan Reilly (9)	175
Verity Young (9)	176
Leah Heath (9)	176
Joel Patchett (9)	177
Emily Blackshaw (8)	177
Jack Barraclough (9)	178
Georgia Lawrie (9)	178
Daniel Hawes (8)	179
Bethan Hurdsfield (8)	179

St John's RC Primary School, Bromley Cross

Carl Cunliffe	180
Nicholas Bannister (9)	180
Luke Bradbury (9)	180
Kate Howarth (8)	181
Matthew Hunt (9)	181
Chania Williams (9)	181
Louise Latham (8)	182
Matthew Deegan (8)	182
Charlotte Brooks (8)	182
Callum Short (8)	183
Isobel Keating (8)	183
Nathan Rothwell (8)	183

Patrick Jarvis (9)	184
Michael Ball (9)	184
Rachel Antrobus (9)	185
Daniel McQuaid (9)	185
Megan Walsh (8)	186
Alex King (8)	186
Jack Corrigan (9)	187

St Mary's Birchley RC Primary School, Billinge

Samuel Gormally (9)	187
Stephen Wiles (8)	188
Liam Baines (7)	188
Natalie Bannister (10)	189
Thomas Harrison (7)	189
Peter Bostock (9)	190
Bob Keegan (8)	190
Harriet Collinson (8)	191
Ellen Gravener (8)	191
Louise Riley (10)	191
Rosanna Owen (8)	192
Archie McCluskey (8)	192
Nicole Friar (9)	193
Alysha Burrows (8)	193
Grant Oldham (10)	194
Samantha Morrisby (10)	194
Elizabeth Logan (10)	195
Elizabeth Bannister (8)	195
Robert Foster (9)	196
Beth Frackelton (10)	196
Hannah Quirk (9)	197
Laurie-Jane Wilson (9)	197
George Collinson (9)	198
Michael Mellor (8)	198
Matthew Frederick (10)	199
Thomas Spencer (9)	199
Beth Howard (10)	200
Jennifer Keane (10)	200
Elizabeth Hague (11)	200
Patrick Lynch (10)	200
Olivia Tickle (8)	201
Daniel Twist (9)	201

Nicholas Clark (8)   202
Robyn Ashby (8)   202
Olivia Mahoney (8)   203
Lauren Halsall (9)   203
Melissa French (10)   203

St Paul's RC Primary School, Feniscowles
Will Ainsworth (8)   204
Eleanor Rawstron (8)   204
Poppy Birtwistle (7)   204
Jenny Parker (7)   205
John Wilcock (7)   205
Marcus Eccles (7)   205
Mollie Beattie (8)   205
Kate Flanagan (7)   206
Benjamin O'Ryan (8)   206
Danielle Cottey (8)   206
Rachael Cross (7)   206
Adam Steven Burgess (7)   207

Sabden Primary School, Clitheroe
Charlotte Wyatt (10)   207
Jack Heywood (10)   208
Leoni Grace Holmes (9)   208
Lauren Bywater (10)   209
Charlotte Knowles (10)   209
Samantha Booth (9)   210
James Smith (10)   210
Joe Wickham (9)   211
Amy Bond (10)   211
Laura Proctor (11)   212
Peter Byrne (10)   212
Naomi Cull (10)   213
Ben Scott (10)   213
Ashlin Orrell (11)   214
Elizabeth Crossley (10)   214
Mary Gill (11)   215

Sudell School, Darwen

Joannah Riley (9)	215
Natasha Tomlinson (7)	216
Georgina Southern (10)	216
Siân-Marie Barlow (10)	216
Shannon Groves (7)	217
Briony Bamber (9)	217
Amy Lucas (11)	218
Siobhan McKenna (10)	218
Sophie Birtwell (8)	219
Jodi Lee Williams (8)	219
Yusra Naweed (8)	220
Tammy Atkin (8)	220
Laura McPhee (10)	221
Shauna Flynn (9)	221
Trevina McKenna (10)	221
Tanya Turner (8)	222
Paige Sharpe (8)	222
Zachary Grunshaw (9)	222
Chelsea Tattersall (10)	223
Kerryn Yarwood (8)	223
Hayley Smith (8)	224

Thorp Primary School, Royton

Lucy Copeland (8)	224
Naomi Slater (8)	225
Demi Leigh Walton (8)	226
Ruth Sudlow (9)	227
Ellis Hudson (9)	227
Taylor Greenwood (8)	228
Catherine Boone (8)	228
Courtney Chappell (9)	229
Luke Hamilton (9)	229
Daniel Hawthorne (8)	230

Walmsley Primary School, Egerton

Anna Blythe (8)	230
Joshua Povah (10)	231
Charlie Bleasdale (9)	231
Anna Hughes (8)	231

The Poems

Love

I give a helping hand to the people I meet,
A smile to make you like each other,
I give you a hand to clutch onto forever,
I will save you a passionate heart,
I chase away your fears,
I give a red rose,
A romantic dinner,
A chocolate heart,
For I am love.

Shauna Dunn (10)
Asmall Primary School, Ormskirk

Winter

Winter is a monster killing the sun.
Freezing the roads.
It is a battle
Raging to war.

The wind is a wolf
Howling in the night.
Killing the sun and heat.
Fire is needed.

Anthony Webb (10)
Asmall Primary School, Ormskirk

Sadness

I make people cry in pain when they fall over
I break your favourite toy
And lose your ball
I cut your knees
And make the flowers wither
I make your ink pen leak on your work
I am *Sadness*.

Emma Hall (10)
Asmall Primary School, Ormskirk

The Weather

He sends a shiver up your back
He is the king of the sky
He howls like a wolf
He will blow anything down that can fly
It is the wind.

He will burn your skin like a fire
He will never let you get cold
He will give you a tan
He has got very old
It is the sun.

Samantha MacRae (9)
Asmall Primary School, Ormskirk

The Mountains

The mountain
Lost in time, lonely
And forgotten by man
Who will find me?
Very few I think

Please someone find me,
Before I erupt
And am gone forever.

Laura Burton-Cundall (11)
Asmall Primary School, Ormskirk

Sadness

I make you cry when you're alone
I make you look abandoned when you've got no friends
I make you go all pale and empty when you're told off
I make you look like a helpless dog
I am Sadness.

Billy Bimpson (11)
Asmall Primary School, Ormskirk

Fear

I am your cold, black blood.
I am the main character of horror movies.
I am the future of your death.
I am the rain that makes you shiver at night.

A soul hunter is me.
I am a monster that scares you.
I make you lonely in your old hollow house.
I am the spider of death.

I am love that disappears into dust.
I am your illness fainting.
My game is 'run'
For I am fear!

Theo Serkumian (10)
Asmall Primary School, Ormskirk

Embarrassment

I make you blush when you rip your pants,
I make you faint in a room full of people,
I paint your face red when you fall off your chair,
And if that's not enough, I make you hang your head
In shame when you forget your homework,
I make you cry when you fall over in public,
I make you feel empty inside when you get shouted at.
I am Embarrassment!

Hannah Bober (10)
Asmall Primary School, Ormskirk

Kindness

I give flowers to an old friend.
I help upset people when their pet dies.
I give food to people who are hungry.
I help a lost dog.
I give love to a cat or dog.
I help a baby that's been left.
I feed a stray animal.
I help a terrified child.
I buy presents for the poor.
I help a widow when you're upset.
I am kindness.

Megan Brennan (9)
Asmall Primary School, Ormskirk

The Wind

The wind is a powerful battering ram,
It is a stampede of bulls,
It clashes against the window,
It pushes the rain in torrents.

It lashes out at people and knocks them over,
It crushes the plants like a steamroller,
The wind whips up the tide and it wakes the waves,
It destroys everything in its way

Nathan Buckley (9)
Asmall Primary School, Ormskirk

Embarrassment

I hang your head low,
When you forget your words,
I tell all your secrets.

I make you blush,
When you trip up,
Or fall off your chair.

I paint your face red,
When you come last in the race,
I am Embarrassment.

Kit Cooney (10)
Asmall Primary School, Ormskirk

Happiness

I am a sunny day,
I am a big dollop of ice cream,
I am a smile on a child's face,
I am a rabbit jumping for joy,
I am a big knot in your stomach
Waiting to explode.
I make you feel loved -
For I am Happiness.

Katie Clarke (10)
Asmall Primary School, Ormskirk

Happiness

I make you smile,
I make you cry with laughter,
I make you giggle every day.
When your friends come round,
You never stop being happy.
When you're sad I always make you smile in the end,
I am Happiness!

Erin Prescott (9)
Asmall Primary School, Ormskirk

Frustration

I make you stressed,
Make you lose possessions,
Give you too much responsibility,
I make you lose your temper in arguments
And later you lose your friends,
Make you feel left out, annoyed,
I give you mistakes that change your life,
I make you feel lonely, miserable,
Pathetic, all on your own.

I am Frustration.

Michelle Davies (10)
Asmall Primary School, Ormskirk

The Wind

The wind terrifies the light.
He bashes through the trees looking for a fight,
People call him the *destroyer*.

He bangs on the window to make cracks,
He scares all the cats and dogs,
People call him the *destroyer*.

He blows flames out,
When he gets angry he bosses people about,
People call him the *destroyer*.

Jake Duff (9)
Asmall Primary School, Ormskirk

Fear

I make your confidence turn to dust,
When darkness takes over the entire body.
I make your mind fill with blackness
And your legs turn to liver.
When I make your happiness fall into the shadows,
When I make all love fade from existence.
I am Fear.

James Barcas (11)
Asmall Primary School, Ormskirk

Guilt

I get people in trouble -
Always caught in the act,
Then in court for them!
Never make you innocent.
I am troublesome,
I can put you in prison,
My name is Guilt!

Stephen Coleman (10)
Asmall Primary School, Ormskirk

Kindness

I give blood,
I heal injured people and animals,
I lend things to others,
I reunite animals with their owners,
I give a smile to someone, who is sad,
I welcome stray animals into my house,
I give away but never take,
For I am Kindness!

Tamaris Higham (10)
Asmall Primary School, Ormskirk

Friendship

Friendship is when you are best friends with someone,
Friendship means you can never be hurt,
Friendship is when you can trust someone,
Friendship is a strong feeling inside you that you can't get rid of,
Friendship makes you gleeful when you are glum.

Charlotte O'Reilly (11)
Asmall Primary School, Ormskirk

The Brain

The brain is clever
The brain is smart.
The brain does everything for you.
The brain thinks for you,
Brains can do what you tell them to.
Brains are big,
Brains are small,
Brains can do it all.
People use them to speak and move,
But they can't do anything without you.

Michael Welch (8)
Booker Avenue Junior School, Allerton

Teacher

T eachers are annoying every day.
E ating dinner and spitting coffee.
A ngry faces all day long.
C atching people and whipping them.
H orse riding every day to school.
E xcited because they like being bossy.
R eady to be bossy to the children.

Marc McLean (7)
Booker Avenue Junior School, Allerton

My Loves And Hates

I really love my PS2,
It gives me lots of things to do.
I really hate Barbie toys,
Just for girls, not us boys.
I really love my Puma straps,
Topped with brilliant clothes and cool caps.
I really hate my mum's mince,
Makes me sick and sometimes wince!
Galaxy is my favourite sweet,
It is the best, it's very hard to beat.
LFC I extremely hate,
EFC are extremely great.
I really love my Sagem phone,
It's cool with a funky ringtone.
I really hate those bad bees,
Stinging you from head to knees.
I really love my nan's tea,
It's so sweet, so warm and milky.
I really hate a belly,
That's fat like my mate Elly's!

Jonathan Southern (10)
Booker Avenue Junior School, Allerton

Stars

Stars, stars every night,
Stars, stars shining bright.
Stars, stars up above,
Stars, stars we all love.
Stars, stars that shine so bright,
Stars, stars all through the night.

Melissa Ellis (8)
Booker Avenue Junior School, Allerton

The Puppy In The Dogs' Home

The puppy in the dogs' home
Wags its happy tail.
Can you give him a new home?
Is he for sale?

The puppy in the dogs' home
He's getting weary.
Please can you give him a home?
He wants you dearly.

The puppy in the dogs' home
He is now asleep.
He dreams of being with you
Make him yours to keep.

The puppy in the dogs' home
He died with no home.
He could have died happily
If he'd only had a home.

Richard Davies (10)
Booker Avenue Junior School, Allerton

Autumn

Autumn is here and there,
Autumn is everywhere.

Autumn is leaves falling off a tree,
Lots of conkers for you and me.

Autumn is a breeze blowing cold
A crunchy blanket of orange and gold.

Autumn is smiling faces,
Wearing old, brown shoes with tattered laces.

That's what autumn means to me!

Beth Tynan (8)
Booker Avenue Junior School, Allerton

The Second Parody

(Based on 'The Passionate Shepherd To His Love' by Christopher Marlowe)

The passionate Scouser to his love.

Come live with me and be my love
In my flat, by the grove
And I will get you Sky TV
And I will feed you KFC.

And we will sit on my divan
Whilst watching cars go by the old van
By noisy roads, which purposes fail
To rid the drivers of their wails.

And I will buy a bed from DFS
And I will get a half-price dress.
A cap of leather, from faraway plains
Embodied with some curry stains.

The noisy trains shall whistle and sing
And wake you early each morning.
If these horrors move your mind
Come to me and I'll be kind.

Jack Davies (11)
Booker Avenue Junior School, Allerton

Sunset Haiku

Chameleon sky
Like a watercolour wash
Shows nature's beauty

Magic vivid hues
Silhouette the darkened trees
And welcome the stars

Crimson-tinted clouds
That could never be painted
A glimpse of Heaven.

Jenny Buchanan (10)
Booker Avenue Junior School, Allerton

The Grey Roof Overhead

She lay a-watching on her back,
She was so still she seemed dead,
As a curtain of rain fell downwards,
From the grey roof overhead.

The day was dull and cheerless,
And full of an unknown dread,
As the rain came falling through the air,
From the grey roof overhead.

She lay in wait of a warm spring day,
And to see the sun ahead,
But the water kept pouring downwards,
From the grey roof overhead.

The days grew old and tiresome,
There was no sunshine yet,
And the drops just kept descending,
From the grey roof overhead.

But eventually, the sun did rise,
And afterwards it set,
The rain had stopped its downfall,
From the grey roof overhead.

Heather Wark (11)
Booker Avenue Junior School, Allerton

Winter Poem

When the coloured days of November
Turn into white December,
They freeze the land
From tree to sand
And the flowers that you remember,
Have gone away
For another day.
They leave the ground bare
And all those that stare,
Are waiting for the plants of May.

Louise Burns (11)
Booker Avenue Junior School, Allerton

Parents' Evening

My mum is in the classroom
While I am locked away
I'm sitting in a corner
This is not a happy day.

And in this little corner
I'm as nervous as can be
It's not a good report
As far as I can see.

Mum opens the door and says
'It was a good report'
She then pulls out a bag and says
'Look what I have bought.'

Sitting in a corner
Is what I do every year
But if the report is very bad
I'll get a kick up the rear.

Michael Rogers (11)
Booker Avenue Junior School, Allerton

Winter

When winter comes the ground turns white,
Away with all the sunshine and light.

The days get shorter, darker and cold,
Which can be dangerous to the old.

Winter has cold biting breezes,
And along with that are coughs and sneezes.

Now the trees are leafless and bare,
While animals keep warm with their extra thick fur.

The gardens are asleep, nothing is growing,
Resting and waiting for spring's seed sowing.

Stephanie Allen (11)
Booker Avenue Junior School, Allerton

The Shark Moves Near

The shark moves near,
Its plan quite clear,
The swimmers move from the reef,
A lot of them in disbelief.

The shark moves near,
Not shedding a tear,
Looking for its prey,
Hooray, hooray, hooray.

The lifeguard comes out,
Very loudly he shouts,
'Move out of the water,'
Too late, he's already caught her.

Remember that tragic day,
When the shark came and took its prey,
And remember always to fear,
When the shark moves near.

David Lang (11)
Booker Avenue Junior School, Allerton

A Poem

The night sky lives in darkness for all to see,
Its beauty is only shown when the moon is at its best,
The sky drifts without a care in the world,
It is only a demon looking on Hallowe'en,
But every night its admirers see it in its only form - beautiful.

James Hall (11)
Booker Avenue Junior School, Allerton

Snowdrop

Only a lonely snowdrop appears at this time,
The bluebells and the daffodils haven't come to say hi!
As winter is starting to fade away,
So the snowdrops are here now to grow and play.

The rain may fall, getting heavier and heavier,
But that doesn't matter, at least it can grow,
As this is going on others start to reappear,
In the field there are hundreds in row by row.

Winter has gone very quickly this year,
And spring is here once again,
Now the daffodils take over.

All the weeds have anchored their seeds into the ground,
So now they can bloom and grow,
Not forgetting to spread and spread.

The poor, poor snowdrops aren't here anymore,
For now there is no space,
For just a small, tiny thing to stay here evermore,
It's such a waste.
It's not so sad if you think about it,
They'll come back next year we hope.

Rachael Spencer (11)
Booker Avenue Junior School, Allerton

Seasons Feelings

I love Christmas, it's my favourite part of the year,
I hate Christmas, it's so lonely and full of fear,
I love Christmas, I get so many gifts!
I hate Christmas, I lie here unsheltered whilst around me snow drifts,
I love Christmas, Dad is busy carving,
I hate Christmas, I'm cold and I am starving,
I love Christmas, it's a time full of love,
I hate Christmas, I pray for help from above,
I love Christmas, can't wait for next year,
I hate Christmas, I wish I wasn't here.

Laura Moran (11)
Booker Avenue Junior School, Allerton

The Lady Of Spring

There was once a lady of spring
And she did a wonderful thing,
She melted the ice,
Made flowers look nice
And stopped all the plants from freezing.

She covered the bare land with grass,
And let the cold winter months pass,
Then sprinkled the dew
And let the weeds through,
Then poisoned the weeds with some gas.

It took a lot of work and time,
Her reward was finding a dime,
She also found money
And buried it in honey,
For other folk like her to find.

Victoria Kendrick (10)
Booker Avenue Junior School, Allerton

My Kenning, About A Cat

Lap-sitter
Mouse-hitter
Night-stalker
Day-walker
Fence-prowler
Moon-howler
Fish-muncher
Bird-cruncher
Hand-licker
Tail-flicker
Milk-sipper
Finger-nipper
Rat-ripper.

Guy Runnels-Moss (10)
Booker Avenue Junior School, Allerton

The Sweet Shop

I walk into the sweet shop,
And what do I see?
Lots and lots of sweets in jars,
Staring back at me.

Astrobelts covered in sugar,
Sherbet lemons, sour and fizzy,
There's all these different kinds of sweets,
They really make me dizzy!

Polos, wine gums and soft mints,
And lots more tasty treats,
I wish I had more money,
So I can buy those lovely sweets.

The shopkeeper smiled and said,
'How greedy can you be?'
'It's not me, it's your offers,
It's buy one, get one free!'

Mars bars, Crunchies, Dairy Milk and Yorkie,
All kinds of chocolate stacked in a row,
Oh dear school is about to start,
But I really don't want to go!

Katharine McCormack (10)
Booker Avenue Junior School, Allerton

Haikus

Winter
Frosted, melting snow
Freezing the cool night-time air
Bursting icicles.

Summer
Blue skies all around
Boiling, bouncing golden ball
Sets the Earth alight.

Pippa Christian (11)
Booker Avenue Junior School, Allerton

What Am I?

Fluffy ball
Extremely small
Night spier
Silent crier
Sunflower seed muncher
Nut cruncher
Cat dodger
Cage bodger
Wheel runner
Acrobatic stunner
Light hater
Patient waiter
Night greater
Paper eater
What am I?

Answer: hamster.

Charlotte Thornton (10)
Booker Avenue Junior School, Allerton

My New Phone

My new phone goes zip and zap,
It sends a message in a flash.

It comes with me from here to there,
It picks up signals from the air.

My new phone has buttons, tiny,
The special finish makes it shiny.

It has the latest game called Snake
It is definitely not a fake.

My phone has Superman on its screen,
He rides across it strong and lean.

My new phone is nice and small,
Oh, and by the way, it does it all.

David Bond (11)
Booker Avenue Junior School, Allerton

Tom The Cat

Tom was a bad cat
He used to scratch
And tear up the mat

He would bite
And kick
He wouldn't miss a trick

But one day Tom went a bit too far
He closed his eyes
While driving a car

As you know Tom was mad
He crashed the car into a shed
Which was very bad

Tom was still since he had banged his head
He was under some wood
And stone-cold dead

Now I must tell you
Something you should know
Don't buy a cat that stoops so low!

Philip Kelly (11)
Booker Avenue Junior School, Allerton

The Rain, Hailstones And The Snow

As the rain trickles down my face, I start to run in a funny pace,
I look down on the floor and see a puddle that goes on for evermore,
Swiftly the hailstones start to drop as they hit the soaked ground
                                                    with a bop,
The hailstones land on my nose, it gives me a tingle in my toes,
The cold gets from head-to-toe I give a shiver and think which
                                                    way to go?
By now I'm nearly home and wonder what the weather is like in Rome,
The hailstones have turned soft, I feel them with a touch of frost,
Then gently the snow falls around, it flutters down to the ground.

Georgia Morgan (10)
Booker Avenue Junior School, Allerton

The Moon

His misty face looks down on us,
His snowy eyes are twinkling.
He wakes above the earth and sky -
I stare amazed - thinking.

Pale cheeks, puffed and chubby,
Look soft as highest clouds.
His lips tinted pink, he smiles,
He laughs, so soft, not loud.

The stars, his friends, I suppose,
Cling round him, shining brightly.
They shine, a pale yellow,
Blended with watercolours, lightly.

I wonder does he have hair?
No, that's silly, he's the moon!
They'd be short grey stubs on top of the sphere.
That was my poem of the moon!

Fiona Boardman (11)
Booker Avenue Junior School, Allerton

The Lion

Jungle king, strong thing.
Meat eater, no cheater.
Beige coat, doesn't bloat.
Large cat, not fat.
Brown mane, not tame.
Aggressive cat, never sat.
Is proud, of pride.
Free feline, not a sea lion.
Huge paws, massive claws.
Eats nice, not lice.
Fast runner, can't be dumber.
Can scare, doesn't care.

Holly Mills (11)
Booker Avenue Junior School, Allerton

Big Sister

She's a . . .
Bossy boots
Never hoots
Clever clogs
Always hogs
Pop chick
Runs quick
Boy snatcher
Heart-throbber
Game winner
All-time texter
Dolphin lover
Mine forever
Animal carer
Chocolate sharer

She's my . . .
Secret teller
Sunny weather
Homework helper
Loudest yelper
Story reader
Baby feeder
Best thinker
Toilet stinker
Pillow fighter
Forever brighter
Favourite flower
Worst frowner
Big sister
Really clever . . .
Our Heather.

Rachael McKeown (10)
Booker Avenue Junior School, Allerton

A Typical School Day

Go to school at half-past eight,
Inside school at nine,
Get my book out quickly,
Everything is fine.

Starts maths at 9.15
Numbers in my head,
I really think it's boring
And wish I were in bed!

Assembly an hour later,
This isn't so bad,
I get told off for talking,
I wish I never had.

It's break now so I'm happy,
But there's still not much to do,
So I'll skip over this, and go on to English,
Is that OK with you?

I do quite enjoy English,
Poetry and stories best,
But what I hate in this subject,
Are all the nerve-racking tests!

Lunchtime is the best part of the day,
Though we do have that canteen queue,
The rest of the day is work, work, work,
I think it's boring, *don't you?*

Now the time we've all been waiting for,
It's just turned half-past three,
I've got to be quick and get home soon,
Or I might be late for tea.

Bethany Leader (10)
Booker Avenue Junior School, Allerton

Animals

Animals big, animals small,
Each have individual strength
Some of them walk, some of them crawl,
But all have a secret power.

All of them can eat and devour,
Before the dawning they rest and daze.
Most retire to their tree bower
And sleep until morning has broken.

Howling and prowling, they pounce on prey,
While other animals eat green leaves.
Nocturnal animals sleep by day
And others enjoy the lovely sun.

Carnivores, herbivores, omnivores,
All are connected in the circle.
Lion cubs come out and scratch with paws,
While a big school of fish pass them by.

Noble sky dancers soar in the sky,
And a baby zebra stands on feet.
Several antelope just passed by,
All linked up in the circle of life.

Joseph Walsh (11)
Booker Avenue Junior School, Allerton

My Friend The Ladybird

My friend the ladybird is small and round and red
You never hear her speaking, not a word is said
She flies around my bedroom and flaps her tiny wings
And every time I see her I think of happy things.

My friend the ladybird has landed on the chair
She is such a tiny creature that no one knows she's there
Oh look here comes my brother, he is going to take a seat
My poor little ladybird is now . . . mincemeat!

Rachel Wignall (10)
Booker Avenue Junior School, Allerton

Haikus

Dolphin
Sleek, shiny, silk grey,
Gliding through the deep blue sea
And jumping so high.

Autumn
A cool breeze flows through,
A sweet, musk scent fills the air,
As leaves gently fall.

Spring
The sun starts to rise,
As the flowers start to sprout,
Peaceful spring arrives.

Francesca Wai (11)
Booker Avenue Junior School, Allerton

No Surrender

A grassy plain green,
Not a soldier to be seen,
The battle awaits.

A grassy plain red,
Shock, horror, all around dead,
The battle was fought.

A grassy plain brown,
As dead as the men mown down,
They battle no more.

Rachel Kelly (11)
Booker Avenue Junior School, Allerton

On The Farm

P igs are smelly
I n that smelly sty
G ulping down leftovers
S melling all the time

C ows have four stomachs because
O f all the grass they eat
W ind blowing through their hair
S melling of good meat

C hicks are very cuddly
H ens are very sweet
I n their little hut
C lucking all the time
K eep on cackling when they lay their
E ggs
N ever break their beaks pecking on the ground
S itting around for hours and hours.

James Harrison (9)
Brennands Endowed Primary School, Slaidburn

Nature

B adgers, badgers
A ll around,
D igging holes in the
G round,
E very evening they come out,
R outing with their pointy
S nouts.

F oxes, foxes
O n the farm
X -raying their prey
E very evening
S lyly moving.

Mick Handley (9)
Brennands Endowed Primary School, Slaidburn

Florida

F lying is a great delight, it is a great view
L ions at Animal Kingdom
O range Lake is my hotel
R ides in Seaworld are very wet
I n hotels they are very posh
D isneyland, you get autographs from everyone
A nimals in Animal Kingdom.

Jordan Gott (9)
Brennands Endowed Primary School, Slaidburn

Goal!

I am good at cricket
But I never hit the wicket
If I wasn't good at athletics
I would be pathetic
I am good at football
'Cause the nets are really tall
And I scored a brilliant *goal!*

David Robinson (10)
Brennands Endowed Primary School, Slaidburn

Nature

The sun is hot
The sea is shiny
The wind is gentle
The snow is cold
The trees are green
The grass is wavy
And everything I see is pleasant.

Alexandra Riley (7)
Brennands Endowed Primary School, Slaidburn

My Scary House

In my big *scary* house
You will see a skeleton in my bath
Count Dracula in my bed
A witch in my living room
And Frankenstein on the computer.

In my big *scary* house
It is always dark and spooky
With ghosts cleaning the floors
And devils cooking food.

In my big *scary* house
You will see a phantom in the car
Wizards watching TV
And a big gorilla playing outside.

Would you like to live in my scary house?

Daniel Parker (11)
Brennands Endowed Primary School, Slaidburn

Dogs

Dogs are cuddly
Dogs are nice
Dogs are cute
Dogs are mad
I hope you like dogs
I like dogs
I give him a toy
He is called Benji
He is cute.

Sarah Tedstone (9)
Brennands Endowed Primary School, Slaidburn

Champion

I have a sheep
It really is the best
I take it to a show
And it beats all the rest.

I have to wash it
Nice and clean
A lot of people say
'It's the best sheep I've ever seen.'

We took it to London show
So I had to stop and camp.
I won the show of course
And I said, 'That's my champ.'

Seth Blakey (10)
Brennands Endowed Primary School, Slaidburn

Polar Bears

Polar bears are soft and snuggly
Polar bears are cute and cuddly.

Polar bears are white
They sometimes fight
They eat fish
As their main dish.

The polar bear you get to see
Might only be on TV
Or you can go to a zoo
And see one too.

Alice Waddington (9)
Brennands Endowed Primary School, Slaidburn

Spring And Summer

Spring is a lovely time,
preparing the barn,
rounding up the sheep
is the sheepdog,
now we are
getting ready for lambing.

Lambs
are lovely
mammals
born in a barn.

Summer is halfway
up the year,
muck spreading
and mowing are done.
Everything is
ready for calving.

Calves
are cute
like little
fluffy chicks
running all around the yard.

Anna Blakey (7)
Brennands Endowed Primary School, Slaidburn

Springer Spaniels

Black and white
Liver and white
Fetching pheasants
Trained to your side
The best gun dog
You can have . . .
. A springer spaniel.

Michael Roberts (10)
Brennands Endowed Primary School, Slaidburn

Snow

Snow is fun.
Sledging down a hill.
Go past a windmill.
There's a field
Full of snow.
Now let's go!

There's a snow show in the town.
Somebody's got the snow crown.
There's a posh lady in a gown.
She's got the snow crown.

Jessica Fogie (8)
Brennands Endowed Primary School, Slaidburn

Football Crazy

One day along came a ref
The crowd said, 'Hey look, it's Jeff!'
He took out a whistle,
Then fell over a thistle
And that's how Jeff got his death.

One day Becks came along
He had a very bad pong,
He ran down the wing
And felt a big ping
And the ball went flying so long.

Along came big strong Owen
He kept goin', goin', goin',
He shoots in the net
Along came Owen's pet
Then he had a shot which was flowin'.

Max Harwood (8)
Brindle St James CE Primary School, Brindle

Snow

One day along came some snow
A man said, 'Oh no!'
He thought it must be a dream
But really it was just a scheme
To get out of having to mow.

One day Max had a snowball fight
When he threw a snowball, it was a good sight
But instead of falling in some flames
It hit his friend James
I think Max was as high as a kite!

Rebecca Baines (8)
Brindle St James CE Primary School, Brindle

Days Of The Week

On Tuesday I went to school
On Wednesday I went to the pool
But one day I did yell
And I was not well
And I felt like a fool.

On Thursday I played the guitar
On Friday I went la, la, la
But my guitar broke
And I had a bad throat
But my mum fixed my guitar.

Benjamin Nuttall (8)
Brindle St James CE Primary School, Brindle

My Dog Lenny

There once was a girl called Penny
She had a dog called Lenny
The dog loved to bark
They always went to the park
And Penny loved Lenny
And Lenny loved Penny.

Lenny had a super great nanny
And Lenny had one called Sammy
Penny was too kind
She had a super-good mind
And Penny never got to see Lenny.

Megan Jenkinson (8)
Brindle St James CE Primary School, Brindle

The Builder

A builder came to our school
I really think he's a fool
But he is keen
In his big mean machine
So now he is so cool.

He came with a load of his friends
He always drives me round the bend
They made some muck
Then he got stuck
Now it is the end!

Jake Davenport (7)
Brindle St James CE Primary School, Brindle

Space Is Cool

David went into space
But he forgot to fasten his lace
When he got there
It was in the air
So he phoned his friend Trace.

Ah-ha space cars
We will fly off to Mars
But wait, oh no
We will go to Pluto
I know we will all have some Mars bars.

Some people said, 'Look at that rocket
It could fit into my pocket
It's as big as a bug
It could fit into my jug
Let's all move back to the cockpit.'

James Gregory (9)
Brindle St James CE Primary School, Brindle

Builders

There once was a builder called Bob
Who couldn't get on with his job
He had to make a pool
Outside the school
But he couldn't because he was a slob.

That useless builder called Bob
He shouldn't have had a job
Because he never mops
He always slops
That's why Bob is such a slob.

Penny Woodhouse (8)
Brindle St James CE Primary School, Brindle

My Magic Box

(Based on 'Magic Box' by Kit Wright)

I will put in my box . . .
My dog digging down
A raft rumbling in the river
Blue's brown and blue eyes

I will put in my box . . .
A beach like a golden ring
A house like a rich owned palace
My parents boring me like Coronation Street

I will put in my box . . .
A cat chasing a dog
And the cat with its bone in its mouth
The sea without water
A dog with scales

My box is fashioned from . . .
Stars and diamonds
With space on the top
And grass round the sides
Water keeps it safe
And a padlock with no key

I will run round my box
Through the sofa cushion
And over the moon
Land on the golden grains of the beach.

Luke Norman (11)
Constable Lee St Paul's CE Primary School, Rossendale

My Magic Box

(Based on 'Magic Box' by Kit Wright)

I will put in my box . . .

My 6th birthday bursting with Christmas Day
a sandy sunset slowly swifting down.

I will put in my box . . .

My old violin teacher like a monkey
my best friend Emily like a caterpillar crawling
my dancing lessons like a kangaroo jumping.

I will put in my box . . .

Riding on a first day at Drayton Manor
my scary roller coaster at school
my first concert going to see air
me floating in the blue

My box is fashioned from . . .

Secrets, gold and stars
and its hinges are like staples
clipped on like super glue.

I shall then go swimming
in the Atlantic Ocean
and when I've finished
I shall lie on the sofa.

Becci Waterhouse (11)
Constable Lee St Paul's CE Primary School, Rossendale

Moon

Moon moon, you are up too soon
Go back to bed, it's still afternoon
Go back to bed and come back at night
And shine your light on us at night!

Natasha Gregory
Constable Lee St Paul's CE Primary School, Rossendale

My Magic Box

(Based on 'Magic Box' by Kit Wright)

I will put in my box . . .

The screaming and shouting noise from a super football match,
The fabulous feeling of flying,
The dreadful disaster of a death.

I will put in my box . . .

The clouds running across the sky, like sheep,
The feeling of swimming in the sea, like a big bowl of jelly,
The excitement of winning a football match,
Like the best Christmas present.

I will put in my box . . .

The great feeling of doing my homework,
The awful feeling when I win a game of snooker,
A white blade of grass,
A green snowstorm.

My box is fashioned from . . .

Oak wood, bronze and stone,
With footballs on the lid and secrets in the corner,
The footballs on the top are claret and blue.

I shall swim in my box,
In a sea of thoughts and memories,
Then sit in a chair,
That is as green as grass.

Adam Smith (11)
Constable Lee St Paul's CE Primary School, Rossendale

My Magic Box

(Based on 'Magic Box' by Kit Wright)

I will put in my box . . .

The swish at night of the sea on the rocks,
In the morning the paws around everywhere,
A rabbit at night licking your feet.

I will put in my box . . .

A horse dancing like me,
My first day at school,
An elephant just born.

A snowman with a dress on,
A model with a carrot on her nose.

On the great view, Mount Everest,
Then canter down onto the golden beach.

My box is fashioned from . . .
Ice, land and polar bears
With dolphins and stars around the lid
Its hinges are the hooves of the horses' feet.

I shall ride in my box
Around my rabbit hutch.

Lucie Greenwood (11)
Constable Lee St Paul's CE Primary School, Rossendale

My Images

(Based on 'Magic Box' by Kit Wright)

I will put in my box . . .

A jolly joke springing out of my mouth
A perfect playing dog to play with
A dumb, dazed, daft dad

I will put in my box . . .

A dancing dream in my bedroom
A correct consecration piece of work
A flitting fish swimming

I will put in my box . . .

A daft, cuddly, new cousin
A dream drawing-cute poster
A fateful, falling, crashing laugh

My box is fashioned from . . .

A crystal locket
A glowing head with jewels sparkling
The secret stuff kept from my friends
The howling wolf clicking

I shall run in my box
In the forest, tripping over branches
Then it should stop
And it will end in my bedroom.

Ashleigh Colquhoun (10)
Constable Lee St Paul's CE Primary School, Rossendale

My Magic Box

(Based on 'Magic Box' by Kit Wright)

I will put in my box . . .

A newborn baby babbling at his mum,
Clasping clouds coming down on Earth,
Green grassy meadows.

I will put in my box . . .

A wedding dress to be a slide,
A viscous dog like a grizzly bear,
The sunrise like a ginger cat
Strolling across the horizon.

I will put in my box . . .

Helping my brother,
Opening presents on Christmas morning,
When my dad into sunrise,
When I was walked into the hospital.

My box is fashioned from . . .

Silent secrets,
It has corners like jungles,
A top of gingerbread.

In my box I shall dive into the waves,
Collect shells from the bottom of the ocean
Then warm my feet in the rock pools.

Jessica Ainsworth (11)
Constable Lee St Paul's CE Primary School, Rossendale

My Magic Box

(Based on 'Magic Box' by Kit Wright)

I will put in my box . . .
shining stars falling from the south
rabbits running round the river
fantastic friends and family having fun.

I will put in my box . . .
ballerinas dancing like elegant swans
horns sounding an alarm, like drums banging away
a birthday like a hot air balloon floating around.

I will put in my box . . .
my holiday in the North Pole
and Santa in Devon
A drawing; black and white
and clouds of many colours.

My box is fashioned from . . .
suns, stars and moons
with summers in the corners and winters in the centre
its hinges are like hair clips clinging tightly to the edge
everything tightly packed, the lid secured by a magnet.

I shall find treasures on sandy shores in my box
then keep them there forever
I'll hide my secrets and my memories
and rest in the light of the moon.

Alex Stokes (9)
Constable Lee St Paul's CE Primary School, Rossendale

I Will Put In My Box . . .

(Based on 'Magic Box' by Kit Wright)

I will put in my box . . .

A sparkly springy sun
A crystal clear cloud
A firework covering the night sky
A mouth full of jokes following me.

I will put in my box . . .

A squashy scrumptious sweet
A dancing deer in my bedroom
A famous flying fish.

I will put in my box . . .

A magic musical magician
A shocking joke out of my mum's mouth
A mucky monkey.

My box is fashioned from . . .
Icicles, magic marbles
Love of my family.

Bethany Holt (10)
Constable Lee St Paul's CE Primary School, Rossendale

Florida

A hot country.
A burning clump of earth.
An excitement giver.
An 8 hour flight.
A theme park holder.
An American dweller.
A powerful pulling power.
What is it?

Lewis Taylor (11)
Constable Lee St Paul's CE Primary School, Rossendale

My Magic Box
(Based on 'Magic Box' by Kit Wright)

I will put in my box . . .
The memory of my magic, marvellous mum,
My doubtful, daft, dainty dad,
My sly, super sister and my beautiful, bothering brother.

I will put in my box . . .
When I finish homework
It's like James Bond cracking a code,
When I cried for my dog it was like a waterfall,
When my dad came back it's like the child's eyes
Meeting the sweet.

I will put in my box . . .
The thump, thump of my first shoes,
The clip-clop of the elephants in India,
The black stars in the yellow space.

My box is fashioned from . . .
Dirty skies painted on its lid,
A crystal clear frame, with elephants carved on its sides,
Its hinges are like the doors on a haunted house.

I shall drive in my box
Up and down the Grand Canyon,
Then bring back a pebble or stone
Or the brownish of the sand.

Alaina Homer (10)
Constable Lee St Paul's CE Primary School, Rossendale

My Magic Box

(Based on 'Magic Box' by Kit Wright)

I will put in my box . . .

A beautiful pair balleting around the ballroom
A lovely lady playing her lovely violin
The everlasting music of many merry pianos

I will put in my box . . .

The silver moon glittering like a diamond crystal
Celebrations like the stars of joy
The love for my brother like the aching heart of a lover

I will put in my box . . .

A hat flying in the pond
Me and my brother playing near our wind
My new niece, Dad
Floating with my aunt and uncle, Mum and Shiza

My box is fashioned from . . .
Snow and silver and peacock feathers
With peace on the lid and love in the corners
Its hinges are the hope and unity of men

I shall dance in my box
On the red and gold horizon
Then drink from the river
Of joy and faith.

Anna Shahid (10)
Constable Lee St Paul's CE Primary School, Rossendale

My Magic Box

(Based on 'Magic Box' by Kit Wright)

I will put in my box . . .

The heavenly Heaven sighted above the horizon
Bouncy dog bouncing beside me
Swimming, splashing sandy sand

I will put in my box . . .

Floating like a swimming swan
Sad feelings like the Devil killing
The countryside as calm as a bird

I will put in my box . . .

A wonderful smile
A first riding lesson disaster

My box is fashioned from . . .

Metal to gold and silver
With stars and moons on the lid
And whispers in the corners
Its hinges are of joyfulness.

I shall ride in my box
On the great mountain tops of the wild Atlantic
Then wash ashore on a tropical beach.

Rebecca Ashworth (10)
Constable Lee St Paul's CE Primary School, Rossendale

Magic Box

(Based on 'Magic Box' by Kit Wright)

I will put in my box . . .
> Grandad grabbing hold of Grandma
> my brother breaking bones
> loving the London Eye

I will put in my box . . .
> My family like a pack of lions
> seeing a TV like a cinema
> me lying like a puppy

I will put in my box . . .
> When I lost the sky
> my blue hair gel
> holiday, losing my mum

My box is like . . .
> A rare bird
> and gold, like
> a crown.

Luke Mason (10)
Constable Lee St Paul's CE Primary School, Rossendale

The Wolves

The fierce figure walked through the midnight trees.
The world shook with his howl.
His eyes were like rubies gleaming with anger,
Looking for his rightful prey.
Silence.
The night was as still as a petrified fish.
It was like peace had broken into the world,
Until it rushed round the forest,
As a signal for his pack mates that prey was here.
Nothing stirred but the voice of the wolves!

Emma Lancaster (10)
Constable Lee St Paul's CE Primary School, Rossendale

My Magic Box

(Based on 'Magic Box' by Kit Wright)

I will put in my box . . .

The sparkling sea shining,
The friendly family having fun,
The dreamy dog dancing.

I will put in my box . . .

My first day I moved here like a sunny day,
My sad thoughts like a cloudy night,
My dead grandad like a miserable day that goes on forever.

I will put in my box . . .

A field of stars
A space full of flowers.

My box is fashioned from . . .
A spider's web
With stripes on the lid and magic inside.
Its hinges are like the lock of a door.

I shall fly in my box
Above the white clouds
Then fall onto a big balloon
That shines with the golden sun.

Sarah Durham (10)
Constable Lee St Paul's CE Primary School, Rossendale

My Magic Box

(Based on 'Magic Box' by Kit Wright)

I will put in my box . . .

A seashore shining silver and gold,
My boisterous dog bouncing along,
A curious blue sky crumbling under cloud.

I will put in my box . . .

A floating feeling like a kite,
My first sight of my cats, small as mice,
My first day at school, terrified as a fish in a net.

I will put in my box . . .

Seeing Missy, my cat,
Chasing Beauty my dog,
My cat with a bone,
My dog with its milk.

My box is fashioned from . . .
Glass, rubies and sapphires,
With planets on the lid and grass on the floor,
Its hinges are mouths,
Filled with teeth.

I shall ride in my box,
On my trail bike in a field
Then get off at the bottom
Of huge, big, green rolling hills.

Andrew Allcock (11)
Constable Lee St Paul's CE Primary School, Rossendale

My Magic Box

(Based on 'Magic Box' by Kit Wright)

I will put in my box . . .

Golden gates glimmering
People silently snoring in their sleep
Festive fireworks flying

I will put in my box . . .

Rows of houses like Lego bricks
Jars on shelves like bottles in a bar
Pianos playing like an army of musicians

I will put in my box . . .
Calling of Christmas puddings
Floating crowds of people

My box is fashioned of . . .
Creaking timber wood
With ashes scattered over it
That seals the box from other people

I shall jump from the sky in Nepal in my box
And will float down to Everest
Then I will climb to the top again and restart.

David Adams (11)
Constable Lee St Paul's CE Primary School, Rossendale

My Magic Box
(Based on 'Magic Box' by Kit Wright)

I will put in my box . . .

The parroting neigh from a pony called Pinny
Floating through the feather-like air
Meeting my faithful forever friend.

I will put in my box . . .

Seeing my mum like a wave of joy
My first day at school like a puppy walking into a new house
Racing on an endless path like a cheetah running at top speed.

I will put in my box . . .

Celebrating Grandad's life and having a party like a funeral
Riding Christmas and celebrating Pinny.

My box is fashioned from . . .
A glass lid to wooden horse heads carved on the sides,
Happiness that overlaps sad thoughts,
It has jewels on the glass lid with glitter that follow behind,
The hinges are glass teeth shimmering from the sunlight.

In my box I will ride a horse called Pinny,
Cantering down from the tops of the hills,
I will reach a beach that has golden sand and seas
That have lots of creatures in,
It will be as clear as a crystal,
Then I will travel with my horse around the happy thoughts
And end back at the beach.

Catherine Hasleden (9)
Constable Lee St Paul's CE Primary School, Rossendale

My Magic Box

(Based on 'Magic Box' by Kit Wright)

I will put in my box . . .

No disastrous diseases,
No wicked war,
A quiet care in this wonderful world.

I will put in my box . . .

My mum, who's like a teddy bear,
My baby sibling, who's like a baby bunny's bottom,
My two baby bunnies,
Who are like my fuzzy bobbles.

I will put in my box . . .

My grandma's having my birthday,
Walking down the dog dying.
The amazing look of slimy snakes,
The horrible look of beautiful bunnies.

My box is fashioned from . . .
Rotten wood, nuts and bolts,
With feeling in the corners,
Stuck with glue, like sticky juice.

I shall hide in my box
My lovely life, my fantasy world!

Jeni Greenwood (11)
Constable Lee St Paul's CE Primary School, Rossendale

Poppies

You're a poppy,
Your scorching redness,
Shines straight through me.

You're a poppy,
Your beauty makes
All the other flowers go floppy.

You're a poppy,
Your wonderful petals
Make everyone happy.

You're a poppy,
You were able to stand tall,
You saw men fall.

You're a poppy,
We admire hope,
You're the symbol which will make us cope.

Ali Asghar Mahmood (11)
Didsbury Road Primary School, Stockport

I Am A Seed

I am a seed and it's dark
I am a seed and I'm hunting for the sun
I am a seed trapped under the soil
But I know that soon my day will come.

I shall grow into a plant
I shall beat the mighty soil
I shall get to the top
But then I shall drop.

Stephen Shackleton (11)
Didsbury Road Primary School, Stockport

A Seed's Life

I am a seed for now,
I'll be germinating soon.
I'll have leaves and a stem
And the most beautiful flower.

But I can dream on for the next few days,
Until my white shoots start to appear
But for now I'm still a seed,
In my pot, in the dark.

I'll soon be reaching high,
My leaves and stem, reaching for the sky,
Then the bees will take my pollen,
And I'll reproduce, to make another one of me.

James McCalla (11)
Didsbury Road Primary School, Stockport

That's What I Do All Year

I start off small,
Then grow, big and tall,
Now I'm a huge beech tree,
I grow my leaves
And disperse my seeds,
That's what I do all year.

When my leaves go dead,
My bark starts to shed.
It all falls off in a pile,
My branches are thick,
My twigs have a prick,
That's what I do all year.

Jack Oswald (10)
Didsbury Road Primary School, Stockport

Journey To A World

Journey to a world,
A world where flowers grow.
Poppy seeds, a daffodil
And a rose as white as snow.

Journey to a world,
With grass as green as emerald treasure.
Even on a desert
A cactus grows with pleasure.

Every country, every world
Has a plant so wonderful, so bright,
So journey to a world
And meet a wonderful sight.

Olivia Cork (10)
Didsbury Road Primary School, Stockport

What Am I?

It's dark and warm.
I'm fighting through the soil,
Reaching for light.
The light is so bright.
I have sharp nettles to protect me.
I live in all seasons.
I'm a gift in Valentine's Day.
I'm beautiful in every way,
I'm a symbol of love.
Soon I'll dry.
What am I?

Ali Keshani (11)
Didsbury Road Primary School, Stockport

I Am Colourful And Bright

I'm colourful and bright
I won't give you a fright.
I'm pink and beautiful
And once again I'm colourful.
I toss my head
In my flowerbed.

I'm strong,
I'm tall.
My friends
Are so small.
I'm old,
I'm always
Being told,
That soon
My head
Will drop
Down dead.

I'm a flower.

Katy Stonehouse (10)
Didsbury Road Primary School, Stockport

I Am A Seed

The shoot began to appear
In search of the warmth of the sun
I am a small seed, I am and I grow
Under the ground and it's cold and damp
And I grow as tall as a giraffe.

A seed.

Georgina Pedler (11)
Didsbury Road Primary School, Stockport

Oak Tree

It was a windy day, I fell from my tree
I hit the ground in lots of mud
Over the years I grew and grew
Humans carved their names on me
I was getting bigger and stronger
I had the sun shining on my leaves
Showing my leaves were all shiny and sparkly
But when campers came and lit a fire
I got scared and it felt like I'd lost my leaves
Until one day I felt a slit at the bottom of me
I fell and fell till I hit the ground
And that was the end of me.

Ryan Williams (10)
Didsbury Road Primary School, Stockport

Holly Leaves

H olly leaves are
O h so spiky, they hurt
L ots when you prick yourself, they
L ook so innocent but when
Y ou get too near. Ouch!

L ots of leaves
E very one as spiky as the other
A ll look like they have
V ery sharp
E dges, holly is
S mall but spiky.

Daniel Quinn (10)
Didsbury Road Primary School, Stockport

Sunflower

It started very small,
It grew and grew and grew,
But now it's very tall,
To be beautiful for you.

With yellow petals like the sun
And dark, dark green leaves,
Beautiful for everyone,
Underneath the trees.

It's not a cornflower,
It's not a rose,
It's a sunflower,
On tippy-toes.

Megan Hughes (11)
Didsbury Road Primary School, Stockport

Daffodil

It was a seed but now it's not
It's a yellow daffodil standing still
It is not small but it is tall
It will grow even more

Grow taller, grow taller
So you can be the tallest daffodil
Grow taller, grow taller
So you can be the most beautiful daffodil

It is the tallest daffodil that's ever been
But soon it will die
And never be seen.

Aisha Mahmood (11)
Didsbury Road Primary School, Stockport

Birth Of A Plant

I am a seed
I cannot deny
I'll love you till I die
Until I say goodbye
But now I am saying hi
And soon I'll have to say bye-bye
So till I die and say goodbye
For now I am saying hi.

James Connor (10)
Didsbury Road Primary School, Stockport

Life Cycle

Once I was a seed
Even smaller than a weed,
Everything seemed so tall
Because I was so small.

Now I am quite high
I can almost touch the sky,
But soon I will die
Why? Why? Why?

Philip Kemp (10)
Didsbury Road Primary School, Stockport

Plants

P oppies have a crown of red petals
L ilies live on water
A nimals like the pollen
N arcissus is the Latin name for daffodil
T omato plants grow fresh fruit in spring
S pring makes the seeds shoot up.

Stephanie Foster (10)
Didsbury Road Primary School, Stockport

The Beanstalk

I'm as green as grass
Growing into the past
I can touch the highest sky
With my long arms high

I can stretch out my bean
And I have a very slight lean
My mouth telling its lie
What am I?

A beanstalk.

Alastair Poole (10)
Didsbury Road Primary School, Stockport

Plants

Plants are beautiful
Plants are cool
Plants are pretty
Plants rule.

Plants make food
Plants make leaves
Plants have roots
Plants grow in seeds.

Bardia Nekooie (11)
Didsbury Road Primary School, Stockport

Flowers

Flowers, swaying in the breeze,
Flowers, embracing the harsh winter cold,
Flowers, as beautiful as can be,
Flowers, sprouting everywhere in spring,
Flowers, relaxing without a care in the world in summer,
Flowers, taking a last stand before winter comes.

Rashpal Cheema (10)
Didsbury Road Primary School, Stockport

Rose

P eople stare as if
L onging to pick me but no one will
A lthough my petals are as red as blood
N obody likes getting stung by
T horns, I'm beautiful
S o everybody says, they call me rose so that's who I am,
    I'm rose, I'm beautiful but will never be picked
               Snap, I've been picked.

Hasina Sattar (10)
Didsbury Road Primary School, Stockport

Growing Plants

Plant pot, plant pot,
Can't you see,
The seeds are ready to grow,
They are going with the flow,
So,
Get your watering can out,
And start watering me!

Callum Hampson (11)
Didsbury Road Primary School, Stockport

Plants

P lants in summer, plants in spring,
L ovely plants all year round,
A ustralia, Austria,
N o one is plantless,
T he daisies, daffodils and even roses,
S un, wind and rain help them to grow.

Joe Parker (11)
Didsbury Road Primary School, Stockport

Flower Power!

I hope my plant doesn't die
It hasn't grown an inch
If it does die, I will cry
I better give it a pinch

It's started to grow
With lovely colourful petals
It's beautiful so
It's as hard as metal

I am now really happy
It's beautiful and bright
Its colours are snappy
It makes me full of sprite.

Jack Whitehurst (10)
Didsbury Road Primary School, Stockport

Snow On The Leaves

Snow on the leaves is white,
Snow on the leaves is light,
Green leaves turn brown,
You can see their dull frown.
But then,
When the snow clears off,
And it turns into thin froth,
Which it does when leaves fall down,
And makes rusty crowns,
Then it melts, melts, melts,
Until then, it's gone.

Mike Oates (10)
Didsbury Road Primary School, Stockport

Year Of Change

Spring emerges its wonderful head,
Saving us from winter's cold tyranny,
And spring's minions had always said,
'Treat us well and we will give you happiness.'

While Spring's minions do their job,
Winter plots his revenge,
But only to be thwarted and made to sob,
As Summer reveals her majesty.

As quick as a flash, Autumn reigns,
With its ageing beauty evident,
Finally Winter's servants go to train,
And Winter rules again.

Jamie Webb (10)
Didsbury Road Primary School, Stockport

Early Morning

Wake up in the morning, what do I do?
The leaves and grass covered in dew
Walk down the stairs and open the door
And enjoy a walk early in the morn

The roses are blood-red
And the tulips as yellow as the sun
Go back inside feeling refreshed
And go back to bed for the rest of the day and night

I can't sleep, go back outside
Everything is different
The owls are hooting
And the beautiful colours have disappeared into the dark.

Matthew Pilling (11)
Didsbury Road Primary School, Stockport

What Am I?

What am I?
I have leaves, a stem
But what am I?
I know! I'm a rose
A lot of people love and smell me
But I'm blue
So what am I?

What am I?
I have small, blue petals
But what am I?
I know! I'm a buttercup
But I'm blue
So what am I?

What am I?
I know! I'm a bluebell
I am a bluebell!

Nicholas Tattersall Baker (11)
Didsbury Road Primary School, Stockport

Plants

I remember the day I was planted
I remember being planted into the dark, damp soil
I remember the soil being scattered over me
I remember it being quite warm
I remember having a little shoot
I remember my shoot beginning to rise
I remember me trying to stretch in search of the glowing sun
I remember the day I was fully grown
I remember turning bright and attractive colours
Guess what I am?

A poppy seed!

Jessica Davenport (11)
Didsbury Road Primary School, Stockport

A Spring Day

Shoots are shooting out of the ground,
Leaves are growing green and strong,
Birds are chirping happily aloud,
Green grass is growing long.

Now the noon's hot sun,
Glistens gently above so bright,
Children are having fun,
Daffodils are such a sight.

The afternoon is old,
The last hour has come.
Night brings cold,
All work is done.

Midnight has struck,
The hour is late.
In the pond there is no duck,
Come again at a later date.

Matthew Ryley (11)
Didsbury Road Primary School, Stockport

Daffodils

I remember being sown into the garden grass
I remember watching an ant go past
I remember growing my first leaf
I remember my roots growing underneath.

I remember growing my stalk
I remember seeing a garden fork
I remember growing my beautiful crown
I remember my leaves slowly turning brown.

I remember when I had died
I remember my mum had sighed.

Stephen Bailey (10)
Didsbury Road Primary School, Stockport

Spring Poem About Plants

Plants are so good, they cheer you up,
Plants smell good and are colourful.
Having a garden - full makes you feel wonderful,
That's why I like plants.

They come in all different sizes, ugly or nice,
The plants can be green.
Some can have a silver sheen,
That's why I like plants.

They can grow in a garden centre,
Where they get looked after.
Some look funny; they are full of laughter,
That's why I like plants.

Lovely trees bloom every spring,
Take, for example, the ash.
Their leaves fall off in a flash,
That's why I like plants.

Jonathan Garner (10)
Didsbury Road Primary School, Stockport

Growing Seed

I remember being planted in the wild grass,
I remember myself growing,
I remember a grasshopper go past,

I remember my roots anchoring into the soil,
I remember seeing the sun boil,

Now I am tall,
I am about to fall,
Falling, falling, falling,

But now I have died.

Mosa Jassim (11)
Didsbury Road Primary School, Stockport

Water Lilies

Floating gently through the water,
Colours of all sorts; red, pink and some green,
Tadpoles swimming by, all keen.

Frogs jump from me to my brother and sometimes they fall,
Making a small entrance to the water with a crash,
Actually a splash.

Fish looking for a bite to eat,
They don't eat from end to end,
For I'm their friend.

I'm as green as can be,
My brothers and sisters are colourful and happy,
But I am not sad, I'm happy,
Even the way I am!

Daniel Parsons (10)
Didsbury Road Primary School, Stockport

The Poem Of The Plants

Long and tall, small and short,
Roots in the ground, flower up above,
Leaves get sunlight,
Roots get nutrients,
Long and tall, small and short,
Bright and colourful,
Dull and dark.
Thick stem, thin stem,
Small stem, big stem,
Green stem, rotten stem,
Long and tall, small and short.

Elizabeth Powers (10)
Didsbury Road Primary School, Stockport

The Cactus

Cactus lives in deserts so hot
Spikes cover it, so animals can eat it, not

Animals there want food from plants
Birds, camels and even ants

The roots travel deep to get their drink
If there's no water they'll eventually shrink

Some are thick and some are tall
Some are thin and some are small

What is the need of the cactus?

They're not used on *Valentine's Day*
They're not special plants, in anyway.

Sami Haddad (10)
Didsbury Road Primary School, Stockport

Plants

P lease help me, it's too cold for me to grow, a
L ittle seed won't survive for long,
A new shoot is growing just next to me,
N ow I wish I'd stayed in the packet,
T oday I hope I'll grow some more,
S ummer will come soon.

P hew, at last I've grown a bit, at
L ong last I will be able to see the world,
A nd then again I'll grow some more,
N ow leaves and petals I shall grow,
T o make the garden colourful,
S oon I will be a flower.

Martine Waterhouse (11)
Didsbury Road Primary School, Stockport

I See

I see life,
With all its energy,
The flowers, the trees,
The honeybees.

I see snow,
Falling very slow,
Like a piece of paper in the morning,
Waiting to be drawn on.

Humour, fun, all the time,
Everywhere.
I see people rushing everywhere busily,
As busy as the honeybee.

I see food,
With a cheerful mood,
I want that mood,
To stay,
As I eat my glorious food!

Adam Corbridge (11)
Didsbury Road Primary School, Stockport

Seed

I am a seed, light and small
In the ground trying to sprout
In search of light and warmth
My roots are sprouting like they should be
Now I'm a flower so delicate and beautiful
I'll never go dull because I'm special
I'm not the only plant that is special
I need care and love to help me grow.

Salman Ahmed (10)
Didsbury Road Primary School, Stockport

Seasons

S oft and woolly lambs are born
P lants are growing long and tall
R eaching up towards the sky
I n the spring a new year begins
N ice and new everything will be
G reen grass with leaves on trees, spring is a time with wind
    and breeze.

S weet summer months with lots of sun
U nder the tree is a quiet place
M eadows and more land, you can see the lake
M any children playing around
E verlasting sun everywhere
R eaching up for the sun, the plants will grow and never stop.

A utumn days have lots of colours
U nder the trees where dead leaves have fallen
T he tree has hardly got anything left
U ncover the leaves, the tree is now bare
M an just looks over the beautiful land
N ever-ending flowers just still but swaying in the wind.

W alking over the snow that is falling
I n the holes are animals, fast asleep
N ever will they wake until a new year begins
T ake a flower that will not survive
E ven though it has nothing to lose
R ivers will take it down, down, down.

Yan Trinh (11)
Didsbury Road Primary School, Stockport

Little Seed

I'm a little seed and I was planted yesterday,
I'm planted in some soft, sandy soil,
I'm a little seed and I want some water,
I'm planted in some soft, wet soil.

I'm a little seed and I was planted yesterday,
I'm planted in some soft, wet soil,
I'm a little seed and I want some air,
I'm planted in some soft, airy soil.

I'm a little seed and I was planted yesterday,
I'm planted in some soft, airy soil,
I'm a little seed and I want some light,
I'm planted in some soft, bright soil.

I'm a big tree and I was planted a while ago,
I'm planted in some soft, dry soil,
I'm a big tree and I need a lot of things,
I've fallen to the soft, dry soil.

Dani Cunningham (10)
Didsbury Road Primary School, Stockport

I Am A Little Seed

I am a little seed
trying to reach the sunlight.
I am a little seed
trying to get out from the darkness.
My flower is growing big and red.
Now you know that I am a poppy seed
wanting to be picked,
and be given to a lover.
I am a little poppy seed
taken care of by a mother.

Aisha Yakub (10)
Didsbury Road Primary School, Stockport

Rose

I was planted in the ground,
I knew I had to be seen,
I knew I was a symbol of love,
I was a rose,
I tried to open my eyes,
I did,
I spread my arms,
And my body, thin as a stick,
My colourful body spread,
I was glowing in the sun,
I knew my life would end,
I would be picked,
I would be picked,
From a girl or a boy,
She or he would give me away,
They would say, 'It's beautiful,'
I was alone,
I wasn't bothered, I was there for love,
There he was,
He picked me,
I was in joy,
He gave me away,
And my life was at an end.

Sophia Georgiou (11)
Didsbury Road Primary School, Stockport

Once I Was Planted

Once I was planted, I started to grow
Once I was planted, the wind jolted me to and fro
Once I was planted, I wanted to get out
Once I was planted, I began to sprout
Once I was planted, I was very small
Now I am big and can stand very tall
But now I am dying, and sighing, sighing, sighing.

Luke Doubleday (10)
Didsbury Road Primary School, Stockport

Leaves And Flowers Through The Seasons

Spring came
Spreading little shoots of green
Little flowers came poking up
Despite the bitter frost.

Spring emerged triumphant
After the freezing cold
But still some bitterness of winter held on
Releasing its grasp.

Summer loomed out slowly
Quite out of character
But soon that was forgotten
The flowers beamed out gratefully.

The roses, the pansies, the lilies
All lazed in the summer sun
Beaming at the children
Running around happily.

Autumn came quite quickly
Compared to the other seasons
The leaves fluttered down
The flowers rotted away.

But the leaves patterned and mosaiced the land
Although the leaves were dead
All the flowers withered
They still lived on as a picture.

James Smith (11)
Didsbury Road Primary School, Stockport

Buttercups

Buttercups make me light up
I like them in the summer when it's hot
They're one of my best flowers, the buttercup
I especially like them when there's a lot
I like it when I shine them on my chin,
My chin goes all yellow,
Although the brightness is a bit dim,
Every time I see one it's like they're saying, 'Hello.'
Then I leave them with a great big sigh,
It's like they're saying, 'Goodbye.'

Megan Whitehurst (11)
Didsbury Road Primary School, Stockport

Different Trees

Big trees, little trees,
Old trees, young trees,
Yellow trees, green trees,
And all of these
Are different trees,
Planted many years ago.
Eventually they will grow, grow, grow,
And even if they pass away
We will still have different trees every day!

Robbie Ford (10)
Didsbury Road Primary School, Stockport

Summer

S now has melted,
U nder the willow tree,
M ore and more start to grow,
M ore and more people start to see,
E ntire ground start to flow,
R ound and round the petals are as children felted.

Mai Vi Giang (11)
Didsbury Road Primary School, Stockport

Harvest Time

I was walking through the golden meadow
Glistening in the morning sun
Farmers waiting for time to sow
Ready for the harvest bun

What a time this will be
For the bakers
And for me
This is the time to become money-makers

I hope this day will never end
Now we wait for Christmas time
And this is not pretend
I love harvest time!

Jack Howden (10)
Didsbury Road Primary School, Stockport

Under The Sea

A mystical beast lies under the sea,
We try searching but there's nothing to be.
It appears and comes only at night,
If you see it, it gives you a fright.

But we still don't go to that place,
Because we don't want to see his ugly face.
He only goes for objects near,
I was afraid, I had no fear.

His scaly body squirms around,
We can hear the noise, it's a terrible sound.
His claws, razor-sharp, claw the sand,
Don't ever reach out he'll grab your hand.

Beware, beware, he eats the fish,
He will even eat a metal dish.
But the last ever thing he ate in the sea,
Was a tiny human, it was me.

Sarah Cole (10)
East Crompton St George's CE Primary School, Shaw

The Box With Locks

As I came home from a cold day at school,
I went to my room and then I felt cool.
My room was a mess so I tidied up,
And that's when I found a box with locks.
I tried to open it but it was too hard,
And then at the bottom of it was a little card.
It read: 'If you want to open me, then use the key
Which is lying right beside me'.

As I looked to my side I saw two keys exactly the same size,
I picked one up and put it in the lock,
But it didn't open the tiny box.
So I took the other key and put it in the lock,
Then I opened the tiny box.
Suddenly out jumped a cute little pearl,
It started to sing, dance and twirl.
'I'm free, I'm free out of this box,'
That was covered with loads and loads of locks.

'Thank you so much for setting me free,
Now I need to go back to my mum in the sea.
So I'll dance my way back, oh yes, I forgot,
There's a ring for saving my life.
I started to stop breathing, I could have died,
She turned around one more time and disappeared,
Oh I wish she were mine.

Rebecca Ireland (10)
East Crompton St George's CE Primary School, Shaw

All Alone

I am alone now,
My friends have gone,
They swam from the boys,
And went away,
Which left me astray,
I sit on a rock and talk to nobody but my tail,
I see my hair flop down my chest,
I feel like I have been let out on bail,
Where I do not know anyone,
And it feels like being wrapped up in rails,
Now it starts to rain,
So the sea laps the shore,
I slide off my rock and slip into the sea,
And go down like a bag of bricks,
I go down to my lair,
And when I wake up, hopefully they'll be there.

Ellis Bradbury (10)
East Crompton St George's CE Primary School, Shaw

When I Was Little

When I was little,
I was a little bag,
When I was little,
I was also a nag.
When I was little,
I was a whinge,
When I was little,
I broke a hinge.

When I was little,
I was in a nasty mood,
When I was little,
I loved yummy food.
When I was little,
Life was all a big joke,
When I was little,
Everything got broke.

Abigail Rennie (11)
East Crompton St George's CE Primary School, Shaw

What Are You?

One dark, gloomy night I was woken
By the sound of my bed being broken
I looked under my bed
Terrified I said
'What are you?
What are you?'

The noise carried on
I was shaking in fear
'Kill, kill, kill'
I was scared, suddenly I heard an eerie spill
'What are you?
What are you?'

I stuck my hand under the bed
Oh, a goblin that's dead
I binned it
Oops, I saw my mum near the bed
'Help me,' I quietly said
'I now know
I now know.'

Andrew May (10)
East Crompton St George's CE Primary School, Shaw

What I Found

The treasure is found and it was only a pound
The king was crowned when he was found
I earned a pound that my mum found
I found treasure, what a pleasure!
We found a thief who was eating beef and gave us grief
I found a flute that didn't hoot
I found ping-pong with King Kong
I found a cable under a table
I wore my vest and I tried my best.

Jason Slicker (11)
East Crompton St George's CE Primary School, Shaw

The Mythical Beasts' Land

T he minotaur stuck in his labyrinth,
H ere's the soul of the dragon,
E verybody's stuck without their souls.

M ythical legends come alive,
Y awning is the minotaur,
T ired he gets,
H earing nothing at all.
I s he just wondering or not?
C alling for a mate,
A ll is lost for the minotaur,
L oneliness he gets.

B e careful of the dragon,
E very time he sways,
A las the roarings of his soul,
S waying to and fro
T ime is near for him,
S oulful in his time.

L ounging is the minotaur,
A ll is calm and well,
N othing will stop them except one thing,
D eath!

Kyle Percy (11)
East Crompton St George's CE Primary School, Shaw

What On Earth?

What on earth are we doing?

Once deers galloped away,
And young badgers hid,
And little squirrels darted
All throughout the day.

Now the forest's a long winding road,
And all that passes through
Is loud, fast traffic,
Where flowers once grew.

Where on earth are we going?

At the end of the lane,
Once autumn days were great,
Our family would go fishing
Using maggots as our bait.

Now the space is a runway,
Everything brand new,
Planes whining everyday,
Where robins once flew.

Ammaarah Vorajee (10)
Gregson Lane Primary School, Hoghton

Pirate's Life

The pirate shoots his gun and drinks a lot of rum
But the pirates don't know that it makes you very dumb
Hoist the anchor, make a banner
Oh no, we need another ladder
When we sing we ding the bell
Then we have a whole new song
All we need is another den then we can eat another hen
After that we go to bed and in the morning we have chips on bread
Whistle the toot - watch out, I'm gonna shoot!

Holly Davies-Hughes (9)
Holy Family School, Sale

Pirate Poem

Yo-ho-ho and a barrel of rum,
Let's go sailing, let's have fun.
Let's go and hunt for the treasure,
Let's go, it'll be my pleasure.
Blood and guts from battle and war,
Even some break their jaw.
On the ship there was a curse,
Lots of pirates needed a nurse.
Help, help, I've seen a ghost,
I'm going to be sick the most.
The cannon ball goes flying out,
Which makes the other pirates pout.
Let's go in the cave that's cold,
Wrap up warm to get the gold.
They make guns go *bang, bang!*
They speak in a way that's slang.
Pirates always want the loot,
Pirates always lose their boot!

Erin-Kate Bonsall (9)
Holy Family School, Sale

A Pirate Poem

A pirate shoots a gun and drinks all of the rum,
They sail their ships and don't like chips,
They look for gold, even when cold,
They fight with swords and don't keep beards,
Isn't it fun? Oh no, he's got out his gun,
Hoist the anchor, push people off the plank,
They feed the sharks until it's dark,
They find treasure cos it gives them pleasure,
They turn into ghosts, no reason to boast,
Not very clever to be as light as a feather.

Nathan Percy (9)
Holy Family School, Sale

The Gun Shoots

T hey shoot their guns and destroy,
H ouses with flames,
E verywhere they

G o! They put down people that are fighting them,
U p and down everywhere,
N ow you want to be a pirate, don't

S acrifice your life and
H ave to be hung
'O w!' each
O ne says one by one,
T hey have the ropes round their necks,
S creaming, 'Help!'

Dean Giblin (10)
Holy Family School, Sale

Pirate Poem

Yo-ho-ho and a barrel of rum,
Sailing the seas, having fun,
Going down I hope there's a crown,
If there's a shark I'll run,
Blood and guts from battles and wars,
People killing and breaking down doors,
'Help! Help! I need a nurse,'
Once there was an evil curse,
The pirates load their cannonball
Bang! Bang! as they shoot,
They hit another pirate ship,
There he loses his boot.

Zoe Coombs (8)
Holy Family School, Sale

Pirate Life

Yo-ho-ho, I've got to go,
I might be back tomorrow,
I'm going on a pirate ship,
Oops I've forgotten my survival kit,
The amount of movement and music,
We might just make a hit,
But if we don't the captain,
Will most surely have a fit,
Yo-ho-ho, drinking lots of rum,
Ooh aah ee I've got a sore tum,
They make their guns go bang! Clang! Bang!
And if you scream you'll now be hanged!

Rachel Lee (9)
Holy Family School, Sale

A Pirate's Life

P eople hate pirates and
 I magine pirates don't have ideas,
R aring to get the treasure,
A fter the fight, they will cheer and drink beer,
T he pirate's life never ends,
E very day the pirate could die,

P irate poems are great,
O ne day a pirate will say, 'Yo-ho-ho and a bottle of rum,'
E very day is a struggle,
M umble, mumble, none of that in a pirate's life.

Thomas Beveridge (9)
Holy Family School, Sale

The Pirate Poem

The pirates set sail across the seas,
Having bottles of rum on the way,
Everyone dancing on board,
Pushing people off the plank,
In every room they have a laugh,
Rum in hands, rum on the floor,
Attacking enemies is their way,
Enemies dead and overboard,
Shaking the other pirates and cheering away.

Liam Conway (10)
Holy Family School, Sale

Pirate Poem

He drinks some rum,
With some in his tum
And sails along his way,
The treasure is here,
So have a peer,
A curse on gold that no one knows,
Skeletons, ghosts and cursed boats,
Listen, listen to the crashing sea,
Come on and have a drink of rum with me.

Ellen Sara Elizabeth Cagney (9)
Holy Family School, Sale

Pirates

Pirates shoot their cannons with passion and high fashion,
They destroy ships one by one while drinking rum
Having lots of fun, acting dumb, beating a drum
Saying 'Yo-ho-ho!'
Cleaning their toes when a parrot's on their shoulders,
A pirate's life forever!

Ryan Cagney (9)
Holy Family School, Sale

A Bug Chart

Blue bugs, moo bugs,
Find them in the loo bugs.

Air bugs, hair bugs,
Find them in a pear bugs.

Light bugs, night bugs,
Fight all for all their might bugs.

Wild bugs, tame bugs,
Shame about their names bugs.

Good bugs, bad bugs,
Really, really mad bugs.

Dead bugs, shed bugs,
They used their claws but
Didn't use their head bugs.

Would bugs, won't bugs,
Do you like them? I don't like bugs.

Alex Berry (9)
Ightenhill Primary School, Burnley

Coming To School

Children groaning,
Mums yawning,
Dads dashing,
Car lights flashing,
Children writing,
Play fighting,
Bells ringing,
Children singing,
Work's mounted,
Numbers counted.

Shannon Donnelly (8)
Ightenhill Primary School, Burnley

Henry VIII

Henry shouting,
Jane doubting,
Mary dared,
Elizabeth's scared,
London crowding,
Monks drowning,
Traders dealing,
Gates sealing.

Thomas Ryland (8)
Ightenhill Primary School, Burnley

The Big Game

Teams trooping
Jamie shooting
Players fouling
Crowds howling
Keeper saving
Kids waving
Big chances
Jamie dances.

Nathan Tattersall (9)
Ightenhill Primary School, Burnley

A Friend

Blue eyes,
Always cries,
Blonde hair,
Very fair,
Yellow shirt,
Big flirt,
Always sharing,
Very caring.

Jamie Catlow (9)
Ightenhill Primary School, Burnley

My Dragon

My dragon,
So gentle and calm,
A keepsake of the night,
A token for adventure,
My dragon.

My mythical friend,
Soaring through the sky,
Bobbing in, out and through the cotton clouds,
My dragon.

My dragon,
Twisting, hot, fiery breath,
Swishing, tango dancing tail and extra sharp claws,
He comes out when the sun is tucked in bed,
That's
My dragon!

Laura Woods (11)
Liscard Primary School, Wallasey

Dragons

A mythical animal floats up and down in the midnight sky,
We think of nothing but rising to the heavens,
We carry on to daybreak and the sun touches the
Dragon's beautiful golden scales.
I sit on the clouds, shaded from the sun,
Only reality can bring me back from this world.
It's hot, vast, red-golden tail in the sunlight
Seemed to give off a heat of its own.
But it itself, was a magnificent creature, bright
Gold and red in colour but was it real or not?
But for now, all I can think about is
Dragon wings.

Danielle Porter (10)
Liscard Primary School, Wallasey

My Dragon

Gliding across the sky,
I can see my dragon in my eye.
It sweeps down like the rain,
Breathing its fire, people in pain.
People watching him over the sea,
He's like the missing magic key.
I got on his back to have a ride,
He's getting ready to do his glide.
I felt I was walking on air,
It was my dragon, I did not want to share.
Under and over the moon,
We will be home soon.
The clouds moving across the sky,
I'm getting worried I begin to sigh.
Dancing like the fire flame,
My neighbours always complain.
The rain started to fall,
My mum started to call.
My dragon has very rough wings,
When he flies past, the wind always sings.
The melody of the song in the air,
Nobody else does care.
He lives in my Wendy house,
He does not make a sound, as quiet as a mouse.
He's like the main thing in my dream,
It's like the sun will never lose its beam.
My dragon, my dragon is the best,
He's even better than the rest.
He will have to go to find his nest,
My dragon, my dragon is the best.

Grace Joy (10)
Liscard Primary School, Wallasey

My Dancing Dragon

My dancing dragon,
Has scales as smooth as silk.
His claws as sharp as a shark's tooth,
His teeth as white as snow,
His flames as hot as lava,
And has wings as wide as the horizon.

My dancing dragon,
Sits on the moon with me in his arms,
He cradles me till the sun rises,
Then he will breath his fiery flames,
That will send light out to the world.

My dancing dragon,
Taps on each rooftop we pass,
He soars through the shimmering mist,
His voice echoes as he sings his beautiful song,
As we float up and down.

My dancing dragon,
Is the best dancer in China,
As he marches along the road,
Waving as he goes.

My dancing dragon,
No one is as beautiful and funny,
No one can sit me on the moon and sing me a lullaby,
No one.

My dancing dragon,
Is gone,
Isn't he.
But he is still in my heart, beating away,
Goodbye my dancing dragon,
Goodbye!

Michaela Johnson (10)
Liscard Primary School, Wallasey

The Dragon Dance

Everybody was tapping their feet,
The dragon was stomping from right to left,
Some children scared, some were laughing,
A blaze of fire, as the dragon opens its mouth,
A roar from the crowd as the music starts,
Looking at clear blue skies but then,
A shower of thunder as the dragon appears,
His dazzling eyes as he turns his head,
Looking at smiling faces that are
Enjoying themselves tremendously.
The dragon's scales shine as a blaze
Of lightning struck the ground.
Waving arms and hands as the dragon
Makes his last appearance.
He reaches to grab the lettuce that is
Hanging from a restaurant door.
Goodbye shout the crowds as the
Dragon fades,
No more dancing,
No more roaring,
No more dragons,
Until next year!

Georgia Thompson (10)
Liscard Primary School, Wallasey

Is It My Imagination?

A crash of thunder in the night,
Like a golden dart,
Shadows darting like a flame,
The thumping of a heart.

Something's coming closer,
I can smell the fear,
Something swishes through the night,
A tail like a spear.

Its breath is as hot as lava,
Its scales are so bright,
They're paved just like some slates,
They glisten throughout every night.

He's yellow, orange and red,
He has some devil horns,
He flies just like an angel,
His claws are as sharp as thorns.

He's not that scary after all,
He is my soul and heart,
I knew him all along,
I knew him from the start.

He is a friendly dragon,
He is my kind best mate,
Or is he my imagination
Or is it even fate?

Jade Wharton (11)
Liscard Primary School, Wallasey

Dragon Fire

Dragon fire,
I thought so lovely as if a dream,
As I soar up to the open sky,
I hear the tail swish and turn,
Like a fish in the shining sea.

Dragon fire,
As he glides swiftly through the open air,
I wonder, is it a dream?
He has sparkling eyes as if they were raindrops,
My dragon carries on gliding past the moonlit sky.

Dragon fire,
My dragon dives down to the sea and rises back up
Like a firework,
He lands on a cloud, a soft cloud,
We gaze as the sunlight dawns,
I wonder, is it a dream?
Only reality can stop us now!

Dragon fire,
I know I will never forget my dragon,
I thought so lovely as if a dream,
All I know is dragon fire!

Callum Rutherford (10)
Liscard Primary School, Wallasey

Dragon

Eyes of fire soaring in the sky,
Roaring and screeching in the misty skies,
Leaping and diving, falling in style,
As storms and rain clouds leap over child.

Dragon
Boiling red eyes,
In colonies and herds,
Orange and red and
Blue and gold flames.

Dragon
Swinging and swirling its
Bright tail,
As a streamlined body
Breathes out dancing fire.

Dragon
Was that a dragon
Or a giant lizard?

Dragon
I watch and stare,
As it glides into the clouds.

Dragon.

Sam Shaw (11)
Liscard Primary School, Wallasey

Why Do Dragons . . . ?

Why do dragons breath fire,
That lovely red flame that I admire?
Why do dragons fly
Up and up, high into the sky?

Why don't dragons walk on the ground
Just like everything else around?
Why don't dragons just catch their prey
Like every other animal catches their prey?

Why do dragons live in caves,
Those black, dark, damp caves?
Why don't dragons just live in the trees,
Away from the honey and the bees?

Why did dragons want to eat us for main course?
And then just changed to the good cause.

I will always remember why the dragons changed to our side!

Ryan O'Neill (10)
Liscard Primary School, Wallasey

My Dragon

One night I had a dream
I was seeing, soaring and shining
As me and my dragon rode to the
Heavens with the moonlight by our side.
As me and my dragon jumped from
Cloud to cloud, I could feel the love
Passing by, with stars glowing in the
Corner of my eye.
My dragon is gentle, my dragon is calm,
With claws as sharp as devil's horns
And don't forget its red fire spraying a sweet smell.
When will this dream ever end?
Maybe it won't, it might go on forever
And ever and ever.

Ellen Cooper (10)
Liscard Primary School, Wallasey

A Dragon From Beyond

Dragon wings,
My dragon, flying up so high,
My dragon's wings fluttering by,
With wings a mile long,
With my dragon I won't go wrong.

Dragon flames,
My dragon guiding me through the night,
My dragon giving us the light,
With fire dancing all around,
With fire as the only sound.

Dragon scales,
My dragon has such lovely scales,
My dragon never fails,
With scales glittering red-hot,
With scales in every spot.

Rachel Hodgson (11)
Liscard Primary School, Wallasey

Dragon

So enchanting,
Empowering,
The magnificent creature gliding, swooping,
As if in a dream,
Soaring over clouds,
Only seen in gaps of blue,
Resting amongst the stars,
Sleeping on air,
So peaceful,
So calm,
Now worshipped,
A dragon!

Liam Roberts (11)
Liscard Primary School, Wallasey

My Starry Eyed Dragon

Dragon Eyes
Swimming through the air, the sky, the clouds,
Is it a dream? No, it can't be,
I can take deep breaths of fresh air,
So I know it's real!

Dragon Eyes
Sitting on my dragon's smooth, scaly back
He's a turquoise-blue,
He's my mythical monster,
My enchanted hero.

Dragon Eyes
We float to the clouds,
We glide forever, it's amazing,
With my best friend, my dragon with me,
We can fly till dawn.

Dragon Eyes
He's left me dreamy-eyed,
Made me inspired,
I love him so,
But I never get tired.

Dragon Eyes
With eyes like starlights,
We float into the night,
With breath so warm,
I can stay here for evermore.

Dragon Eyes
With teeth like Jaws,
Big as an elephant,
Strong as a horse,
All I dream about is
My starry-eyed dragon!

Chloe Cunningham (11)
Liscard Primary School, Wallasey

Dragon Wings

Dragon wings,
I thought so lovely,
To glide over and under clouds,
What a thought to walk on air,
Dragon wings,
As long as I can see,
I reached out and touched my dragon,
His scales were as hard as iron,
My dragon started to slow,
He stopped and sat on a cloud,
I climbed down from his back and
Sat next to him.
Dragon wings,
He started to flap his wings,
Cloud covered my eyes,
I was blinded by the cloud,
When the cloud cleared,
My dragon was gone and
I was back on the ground,
Just a dream, or was it?

John McAfee (11)
Liscard Primary School, Wallasey

My Dragon

One night I saw a dragon
Who lived under the stairs
I saw him breathing fire one day
I thought they lived in lairs!

He went out flying in the middle of the night
I saw his orange shade
A ball of smoke came out his snout
His fangs can dig just like a spade.

He finally came down to sleep in the grass
A long tail curled around him
I could not see his blinking eyes
For the moonlight was so dim.

He stood up with legs like tree trunks
As tall as a house
His tiptoeing fire danced around me
As quiet as a mouse.

An orange wing came down to greet me
And lifted me onto his back
We soared high up into the clouds
I should have brought him a snack!

As we came down to the house
I cried out to my mummy
'I have a new pet dragon now,
Can we call him Sunny?'

Danielle Hall (11)
Liscard Primary School, Wallasey

My Dragon

My dragon,
An amazing creature,
Soars high as Heaven, through cotton wool clouds,
The sun beating down on blood-red scales,
This beautiful creature flying towards the horizon.

My dragon,
Sails through the clear blue sky,
On mile-long wings, with the talons
Of an eagle as sharp as piranhas' teeth
And bulging red eyes like fireballs in
The midnight sky.

My dragon,
When the morning comes alive and the sun awakes,
My dragon's wings unfold and will glide forever
And a day over land and sea and the sun shines
And reflects off the water to shine on us.

My dragon
Has fierce fangs - pure white, a million
Of them and a whipping tail with spikes
Down his long spine.

My dragon: a guard to keep me safe at night
And a ticket for a new adventure.

Jonathan Addyman (10)
Liscard Primary School, Wallasey

Dragon

Is this real?

As we glide through the clouds,
My dragon's scales glisten in the midsummer sun,
The warm breeze passes my ears with a thrust,
I thought it would be scary but it's fun.

Is this real?

We are seeing, soaring and shining as we rise
Into the heavens,
He opens his wings out wide and we glide on
Forever, getting higher each time,
I think we're about sixty-seven feet high now.

Is this real?

It's getting late,
The stars are coming out,
I should go home now but I doubt,
We fly on back,
I thank him for the ride
And wake up.

I wish it was real!

Sarah Finnigan (10)
Liscard Primary School, Wallasey

My Special Dragon

My special dragon,
It's like a dream come true,
Soaring high in the sky,
He wouldn't hurt a fly,
It's starting to get late,
The sky's really dark,
All I can see are the lights in the park,
I start to worry so my dragon
Goes out in a hurry,
We fly past the moon
And all the stars, we're
Nearly there, I think I can see Mars,
My dragon gets ready to do his glide,
I'm wondering how much I would have missed
If I hadn't gone on this ride,
We swoop past a wall
My family starts to call,
Me and my dragon land on the ground,
I look around,
I say goodbye to the dragon that left me dreamy-eyed,
I hope I'll see him again soon
As I look out the window in my room.

Lisa Kinnear (10)
Liscard Primary School, Wallasey

Dragon's Party

Dragon's dancing,
Dragon's diving.

Tails swishing as the music plays,
Scales shining in the sun,
They haven't felt this for days,
They are having so much fun.

Dragon's dancing,
Dragon's diving.

Music playing like a bird singing her favourite song,
This party's gonna last all night long,
Breathing, bouncing fire to the clouds dancing by.

Dragon's dancing,
Dragon's diving.

Wishing wonders to the wind,
Party poppers banging to the beat,
While dragon's move their feet.

The time has come for the dragons to
Stop dancing and diving,
If you listen closely you'll hear them
Having another party!

Natalie Eastwood (10)
Liscard Primary School, Wallasey

The Dragon

The dragon
Like a shooting star across the midnight sky,
The dragon takes me higher and higher.

The dragon,
As he took me high up and up
The glimmering sun shone down on his sparkling scales,
Yet we still go higher and higher until my ears
Burst, then finally we land on a cloud
As fluffy as cotton wool,
We rest, the dragon's breath a mist, like smoke
To keep us cool and when I'm cold
He will breathe a dancing fire to keep me warm,
The dragon
I long for my dragon to stay with me,
Forever together we will always be,
My dragon and me!

Gemma Wright (11)
Liscard Primary School, Wallasey

My Special Friend

I thought so lovely of my dragon,
When the sun beats down on its glittery
Hot scales with claws like sharks' fangs
And scales of a fish, we see the mythical town
Of ancient China but we carry on to the
Heavens, he brings out an enchanting flame
Of dancing dragons sailing on the pillows of air,
The silver-eyed moon watches over us and
Showers us with lightning rays which wash
My troubles away, it's a dream to you, but is it to me?

Lewis Simpson (10)
Liscard Primary School, Wallasey

My Dragon

My dragon,
Soaring through the clouds like a fish in the sea.

My dragon,
Swiftly gliding to meet me.

My dragon,
With wings as wide as a house.

My dragon,
Breathing fire from his snout.

My dragon,
Glittering scales in the sun.

My dragon,
Together we have loads of fun!

My dragon,
Straying in and out of time.

My dragon,
Shalt not commit a crime.

My dragon,
All mine no one else's.

Connor Wray (11)
Liscard Primary School, Wallasey

Dragon?

Looking down on the land,
The sky making it look like
I was floating over a land of sapphire,
The dragon stretching its wings and
Tail as we glide through the air
And then out of nowhere the
Black dragon of the skies
Hurtled towards us like a missile
From a submarine.
It stopped in front of us and its
Glittery black scales glistened
In the moonlight.
My dragon whipped its tail at the sky
Dragon and sent it hurtling towards the ground,
We set off only then to be caught up in a storm!
'Argh!'
I screamed,
Whoosh,
We'd been sucked up by a tornado
The grey and white colours swirling round
Like a spinning top.
I looked up and saw the clouds move
Slowly round one at a time
Then eventually disappeared.
Roar! My dragon yelled and we pushed our way
Through the barricade of mud and
Dust until we got to the other side,
My dragon was now weak and battered,
We were falling,
My dragon was dead.
'Dragon!' I screamed!

Owain Pierce-Hayes (10)
Liscard Primary School, Wallasey

Dark Dragon

The dark and powerful beast
Dwelling in the gloomy, murky underground,
Crying out with its glorious growl,
Surely this magnificent animal
Should not be imprisoned?
The Earth shakes,
The ground breaks,
Its broad wings open
It's gone,
The creature's tough scales
Moisten as it glides through the clouds
And lets out its fatal flame
To let the world feel the pain itself had felt,
Everything on Earth was in ruin,
From the tallest mountain,
To the smallest sea,
The dragon had won!
The world as we know it was dead.

James Harrison (11)
Liscard Primary School, Wallasey

Bike Riding

Legs aching,
Dehydrating,
Pedals turning,
I'm just learning,
It's so tiring,
Can't stop pedalling,
Riding round,
Then I found a puncture in my tyre,
Because I ran over some barbed wire,
Legs aching,
Dehydrating,
Pedals turning,
I'm just learning.

James Hammond (10)
Lostock Gralam CE Primary School, Northwich

In The End

One day I let you out,
I called for you, you weren't about,
Then I found you on the ground,
No movement and no sound.

I remember when you would talk to me,
Even though I didn't know what you'd say,
You would purr when you wanted to eat,
Then I would give you a treat.

In my dream, I saw your face,
I woke up, there wasn't a trace,
I thought of you in my head,
As if you were there, on my bed.

Now you're gone I'm alone again,
I'm trying not to show the pain,
But in the end you've got to go,
I only have a picture to show.

Ben Cooper (10)
Lostock Gralam CE Primary School, Northwich

P J Bear

On Monday he jumps into bed,
On Tuesday he plays a game,
On Wednesday he rows a boat across a lake,
On Thursday he charges down some stairs,
On Friday he watches out of the window,
On Saturday he packs away his stuff,
On Sunday he finds himself in a big bin lorry.

Matthew McKechnie (10)
Lostock Gralam CE Primary School, Northwich

Houses

Number 5 is a happy old lady,
Short and plump, with rings of flowers,
Relaxing in sunlight,
With her dangling earrings of gems

Number 7 is a sad old grandad,
Sitting in a sad old city,
Old but sturdy,
Big box glasses.

Number 9 and 11,
Siamese twins with sparkly dresses,
Twinkly tinted eyes,
Sparkly earrings.

Number 13 is a tall basketballer,
With a black face,
No hair, bare,
All alone.

Number 15 is an old window,
No jewels just wrinkles,
Lost her husband,
No one to care for her.

Liz Atherton (10)
Lostock Gralam CE Primary School, Northwich

Houses!

Number 5 is an old short and stumpy granny,
With huge square glasses
Wearing her favourite twinkly bracelets
And a round belly.

Number 7 is a young independent man,
Tall and sturdy,
Its face is long and a square jaw,
With lanky pale arms.

Number 9 and 11, are two teenage best friends,
Very reliable on each other
And have long brown hair
And sparkly earrings.

Number 13 is a tall and narrow grey woman,
With small, round glasses, a bumpy nose
And long pointy fingers.

Number 15 is burnt, black and bald,
Died in a fire,
Memories of red flames
And burning face.

Donna Edwards (11)
Lostock Gralam CE Primary School, Northwich

Houses

Number 5 is asleep,
Looking at children leap,
There goes the milk tooth,
Blood falling on her beads.

Number 7's veins are out,
Blood is running all about,
Germs are flying all around,
Taste buds wild.

Number 9 and 11 love each other,
They are sister and brother,
Their mum and dad live across the road,
Their numbers are 10 and 12.

Number 13 is a tall, thin man,
On his head is a steaming pan,
He has cracks in his face,
Putting on his clothes.

Number 15 dropping tears,
It has no more fears,
Empty belly,
Now it is dead.

Daniel Kenneth Grannell (11)
Lostock Gralam CE Primary School, Northwich

Houses

Number 5 has a locked jaw,
The face is crackled and pale,
A fairy cake with a cherry in the middle,
With a necklace around the neck,
With a stiff cemented back.

Number 7 is a big detached house,
With a cemented back that can't move,
With glasses to deflect the sun,
With jam tarts laid out on a tray.

Number 9 and 11 are a stout old lady,
With cracks in her face but twinkled eyes,
Sprawling comfortably
And wearing her brightly-coloured beads with pride.

Number 13 is a tall and narrow, detached house,
Called a country house,
It has four floors,
All nice and posh.

Number 15 is an empty house,
All alone and by itself,
Crying for someone to play
And has no friends.

Ryan Whitlow (10)
Lostock Gralam CE Primary School, Northwich

Ben!

We had great times together,
Me and Ben running about,
We got told off together,
Especially when Dad was the one to shout.

I always spared you some crackers,
When we were watching Coronation Street,
I love to stroke your fur,
Sitting on the dining table seat.

It was so much fun,
When we made dens,
With loads of sticks,
Behind your dirty pen.

But now you've gone to your grave
And I'm so sad,
We've buried you in the garden,
Me, Amie, Mum and Dad.

I wish you hadn't gone,
In my heart you are a treasure,
When I come home,
You were my leisure.

I really, really miss you,
When you escaped,
Jumping over the gate,
Like a giant ape.

You scratched the door,
When it was firework night,
So I'd hold you in my arms,
Very, very tight.

But never again!

Hannah Thorp (10)
Lostock Gralam CE Primary School, Northwich

Pupil

Carpet sitter,
School hater,
Naughty worker,
Outside skater.

Handwriting neater,
Lousy worker,
Pencil trimmer,
Toilet lurker.

Music lover,
Brilliant swimmer,
Nail biter,
Race winner.

Playtime lover,
Art drawer,
Home time lover,
Fingers sore.

Ian Hindmarch (10)
Lostock Gralam CE Primary School, Northwich

Sadie

I remember when my grandma told me
About a cat who stole my dummy,
Her name was Sadie,
Who was a beautiful lady,
Me and her played together a lot,
I hope you remember me, forget me not.

Sadie, I wish you could come back to me
And then I can sit you on my knee.
I remember when you sat under a tree
And near the fire, right near me.
I stroked you and stroked you
That was then,
I think that you will be amazed,
Because I am now ten.

Megan Morrell (10)
Lostock Gralam CE Primary School, Northwich

Woodland Cinquains

In spring,
Trees turning green,
New buds starting to grow,
Buds starting to form on the trees,
New life.

Summer,
Bright as the sun,
Animals in the wood,
All the flowers then brighten up,
Sunshine.

Autumn
Brown, crispy leaves,
The branches go mouldy,
The weather starts to get colder,
Leaves fall.

Winter
Weather is cold,
Animals are in bed,
The tree tops are covered in snow,
Good year!

Jonathan Lightfoot (11)
Lostock Gralam CE Primary School, Northwich

Pupils In School

Hard worker,
Nose picker,
Spelling learner,
Bogey flicker.

Music lover,
Troublemaker,
Playground lurker,
School hater.

Swimming winner,
Nail biter,
Wasting dinner,
Sum writer.

Carpet sitter,
Best dancer,
Rubbish pointer,
PE prancer.

Brilliant maths,
Good timetables,
Always naughty,
Picking labels.

Philippa Cavanagh (10)
Lostock Gralam CE Primary School, Northwich

Pupils

Great helper,
Hard worker,
Ear listener,
Best shirker.

Pencil writer,
Classroom concentrator,
Teacher watcher,
Rain hater.

Merry smiler,
Chitter chatter,
Nail biter,
Pen splatter.

Fast typer,
Playground hopper,
Team encourager,
Disco bopper.

Challenge warrior,
Getting better,
Determined shooter,
Writing letters.

Conor Hardman (10)
Lostock Gralam CE Primary School, Northwich

Football

Legs aching,
Back breaking,
Dehydrating,
Can't stop waiting,
Eyes on ball,
Free-for-all,
Head for goal,
Mind the hole,
Ball flying,
Time dying,
Get set,
Ball in net,
Half-time,
Drinking time,
Back on pitch,
Someone rich,
Legs aching,
Back breaking,
Dehydrating,
Can't stop waiting.

Bradley Sutton (10)
Lostock Gralam CE Primary School, Northwich

Woodland Cinquains

The spring
Trees are spreading,
Buds are breaking into shapes,
Trees are showing hints of green leaves
End spring.

Summer
Hot, scolding sun,
Leaves are red and brown colour,
The trees are going very bare,
New life.

Autumn
Is very warm,
With breezy and cold air,
With flowers growing everywhere,
New life.

Winter
Cold and windy
Thundering and lightning,
Children keep themselves so cosy.
The End.

Sam Illidge (11)
Lostock Gralam CE Primary School, Northwich

Woodland Cinquains

In spring,
Leaves start to grow,
Birds start to build their nests,
The trees grow higher and higher,
New life.

Summer
Starts to get hot,
The flowers start to grow,
The leaves get ready for autumn,
New life.

Autumn,
Leaves fall off trees,
Leaves on trees are yellow,
They slowly fall down in the wind,
New life.

Winter
Snowflakes falling,
Animals are asleep,
Treetops are covered in snowflakes,
New life.

Ben Dean (10)
Lostock Gralam CE Primary School, Northwich

Jesse

The first time I met Jesse
So soft and cuddly
Playing tug of war
Peeping out the wooden door.

Playing fetch with her ball,
Taking photos of her on my lap,
Her tongue wet and sticky,
Playing Christmas songs all night,
Always used to make her bark.

As time passed slowly,
She was growing old but never stopped playing,
One day she died of arthritis,
I stopped dead and cried.

My memories of her made me sad,
She died, in my memory I thought she was alive,
But now she's gone to a great place called
Heaven.

Looking at a photo of her,
Still makes me cry,
So she is in my memory
And I'll never forget her.

Daniel Johnson (9)
Lostock Gralam CE Primary School, Northwich

Seasons

The spring
Call out the buds
Which all come out of the ground
Now the flowers have grown and sprung
New life.

Summer
It is really hot
Animals run around
The sun goes down to the next day
New season.

Autumn
Leaves fall
Children playing climbing.

Bird berries grow
Animals gather nuts
Months over.

Winter
Winter days
Snow covers the ground
Sliding down a hill
Snow stops
New year.

Phillip Clark (11)
Lostock Gralam CE Primary School, Northwich

The End

My mum bought me a pet,
A golden retriever,
We called him Sparky,
He was as good as gold.

His jet-black eyes and soggy wet nose,
Playing games and races,
He always won,
Fast as someone after gold.

Taking him on walks,
He loved fetch,
I tried to beat him,
It was great.

Until the day,
You gashed your neck,
On a rusty pipe,
He dropped and died.

Sat in my chair,
With no friend,
Cold arms,
No neck to put them round.

Jack Canniffe (10)
Lostock Gralam CE Primary School, Northwich

Woodland Cinquains

The spring,
Buds start to form,
They burst from brown branches,
The leaves start to come on the trees,
New start.

Summer,
The sun comes up,
The flower buds come up,
All the leaves turn to green again,
Hotter.

Autumn,
Green, yellow, brown,
Leaves start to fall off trees,
It's coming - winter, cold again,
New start.

Winter,
Winter is cold,
Snow starts to fall slowly,
White all around on the cold floor,
New life.

Joanne Cragg (10)
Lostock Gralam CE Primary School, Northwich

Houses

Number 5 is a big chubby lady,
With lines so dark coming from her face,
Sprawling comfortably,
All gold and beady.

Number 7 is a long, stretched, yellow house,
It wears sparkling wide glasses,
Drums lined up all sparkly and clean.

Number 9 and 11 are two twins
With food being shoved in their mouths,
With large shiny eyes,
Gleaming in the sun.

Number 13 is a tall thin tree,
With massive, massive hair,
His large red lips
Shine in the light.

Number 15 is a big, fat, empty belly,
It's got a really bad feeling
And all the flowers are going up to Heaven
The house has collapsed.

Michael Perry (9)
Lostock Gralam CE Primary School, Northwich

Woodland Cinquains

The spring
Brings in new life,
The plants burst from their buds,
There are little leaves on branches.
New life.

Summer
Summer is hot,
New plants start coming up,
The children play in the bright sun.
New life.

Autumn
Leaves fall from trees,
Bare trees and old stay still,
The grass is buried underneath.
New life.

Winter
Winter is cold,
The road is blocked with snow,
The children play in the white snow.
New life.

Victor Depenha (10)
Lostock Gralam CE Primary School, Northwich

Pupils

Teacher register,
Maths dummer,
Hard worker,
Literacy hummer,
Playground lurker,
Eating dinner,
Nail biter,
Holy sinner,
Arts drawer,
Getting fitter,
Bell ringer,
Chair sitter,
Music lover,
Here's break,
Clock ticker,
Eating cake.

Joel Evans (10)
Lostock Gralam CE Primary School, Northwich

Wonderful Weather

As a bolt of lightning crashes,
My windowpane smashes.
The wind starts to blow
And the thunderstorm will go.

The sunshine comes out,
The birds begin to sing.
They have beautiful patterns
On their little wings.

The dark clouds are coming,
Hovering overhead.
The rain starts fall
And everything goes dead.

Christian Richardson (10)
Marsh Green Primary School, Wigan

Alphabet

The alphabet has A, B, C,
It doesn't have 1, 2, 3.
It has 26 letters,
Come and read with me.

The alphabet is fun to read,
Come and read with me,
If you don't you'll miss out on the fun.
So please just read with me.

Teachers talk about the alphabet,
And say that it is cool.
They teach people to read it,
And make poems with it too.

So come and read the alphabet,
It is very cool and fun.
I guarantee you that
You'll never be alone.

John Neville (10)
Marsh Green Primary School, Wigan

Once Upon A Rhyme

The silver lining of the moon
colourful planets and thick gloom.
In the rocket flying through space,
then we started speeding up the pace.

Blasting-off from the ground
and made a powerful sound.
Dodging and weaving through the stars
and saw a rocket land on Mars.

Seeing the little old Earth
but still remembering where my mum gave birth.
I see the sun and the clouds
making NASA extremely proud.

Kieran Dixon (10)
Marsh Green Primary School, Wigan

My Tiny Dog

My dog is teeny-weeny,
Like a little tiny ant.
He is very friendly,
Very soft and fluffy.

My dog is very cute,
Like a beautiful flower.
He walks around
To the backyard.

I take him for a walk,
He drags me and pulls me.
He runs onto the grass,
And digs holes deep.

My dog can be fierce,
He rips slippers to bits.
Digs a hole
And puts your T-shirt in it.

My dog can be friendly,
Chasing me around the room.
My dog goes in his basket
And goes to sleep quietly.

Adam Hunter (10)
Marsh Green Primary School, Wigan

Untitled

There's a monster that lives in the toilet,
His name is Loopy Loo.
He's green and blue and camouflaged
To look like nasty poo.
He lives down in the sewer,
He only comes up at night,
To scare people in the bathroom.
He give them a fright.

Robyn & John
Marsh Green Primary School, Wigan

Not My Shoes

Not mine, too hard,
Not mine, too bumpy.

Mine were a comfy pair of slippers.

Not mine, too stinky,
Not mine, too black.

Mine smelled like bright red roses on a summer's morning.

Not mine, too messy,
Not mine, too dirty.

Mine are very clean, very, very clean.

Not mine, too lumpy,
Every time I wear them my toes screw up.

But mine were just right.

Not mine, too damaged,
Not mine, too wet.

Mine were new.

Not mine, too dull,
Not mine, too old.

Mine were only one month old.

Not mine, too big,
Mine were just the right size.

I wish! I wish! I'd left my own on my two feet.

Dionne Forshaw (10)
Marsh Green Primary School, Wigan

Inside My Friends Lucy And Kate

Inside my bestest friends Lucy and Kate
Are two cats fighting like a pair of lions.
They sleep through the day and go wild at night.
It's like at night, when their mum and dad call them
They hide and ignore them.
They are the twins of the street,
They are never off their feet.
When they are angry they claw you.

Sometimes they're funny,
Sometimes they're boring.
One of them is fat
And one of them is skinny.
They're my best friends ever.
They play with me every day.
When they return from their learning,
Sometimes my friends are considerate
And helpful and never look like they're fighting.
Kate's got long hair and Lucy has short curly hair.
They have a brother called Ben.
They are my bestest friends in the world ever!

Sarah Louise Dawson (10)
Marsh Green Primary School, Wigan

Untitled

When you are quietly sleeping,
He creeps into your room.
He's looking out for spectacles,
He grabs, then out he zooms.
He really needs those glasses,
Because he cannot see.
He also needs some false teeth,
He won't get them from me.

Dale
Marsh Green Primary School, Wigan

Kangaroo

My little baby joey
he hops around
making no tiny sound.
Sleeping inside his mother's pouch
it is as comfortable as a couch.
Playing happily as he can be,
just because he can see me.

Baby joey is the smallest of the lot,
on his left ear he has got a black spot.
His mum is very caring,
she's got a heart of gold.
We care for her as we care for joey.
Happily they live their lives
in the Australian countryside.

Kelly Sharpe (10)
Marsh Green Primary School, Wigan

When I Grow Up

When I grow up I want to be a pop star with lots of money.
When I grow up I want to be a football player with a very fast car.
When I grow up I want to be rich and famous with a servant in
every room.
When I grow up I want to be a lumberjack with a very loud voice.
When I grow up I want to be a scientist with an inventive mind.
When I grow up I want to be a mathematician with a large brain.
When I grow up I want to be a racing car driver with a very big garage.
When I grow up I want to be a teacher with a very small class.
When I grow up I want to be a poet with a lovely brain.
When I grow up I want to be a cashier with a loving family.
When I grow up I want to be a gangster with a very strict gang.
When I grow up I want to be me!

Paul Marcroft (10)
Marsh Green Primary School, Wigan

The Bird

The bird is amusing
He flies in straight lines.
He's fast, you could never capture him.
Even if you tried your best
You still could not capture him.
When he flies you think he's slow
But he's really fast indeed.
He lands very smoothly on the hard gravel.
When he eats, he gobbles it up very quick.
He lives in trees.

Birds are scared of cats, dogs, people and snakes.
There are all kinds of birds like pigeons, parrots, herons,
blackbirds and kingfishers.
The kingfisher is the only bird that can swim underwater.
The colour of the kingfisher is green and red.
It eats fish, worms and maggots.
It eats six times a day until it dies.
Its eggs are very small.
When the eggs hatch,
The bird's head pops out of the egg
Like a worm popping out of the earth.
When the chick learns how to fly and swim underwater
The baby bird no longer needs its mum or dad.

Leon Speakman (10)
Marsh Green Primary School, Wigan

Winter Is Departing

I am the frost,
I put ice on windows,
Spreading around the streets,
Giving people cold, wet feet,
Cold noses, sad faces.

Sparkling cobwebs,
Icy wind,
All around the city street,
Slippery floors,
And icy doors.

Frosty windows,
Sliding on the ice,
Winter's moon with frosted rings.

When the sun rises,
There are lots of surprises.
All the ice melts,
Winter has departed,
That was the best one
That I have ever had.

Robert Robinson (10)
Marsh Green Primary School, Wigan

My New Puppy

My mum got me a new puppy,
She said it was all lovely,
It jumped around,
And turned around,
But soon I would beat her in a round.

My puppy is all fluffy,
She is very cuddly,
We play around
All night and day,
But when I go to get her
She's under the hay.

My puppy sleeps all softly,
But she never sleeps as she creeps.
When she goes for a drink
She always makes a tink
But I love my puppy
Because she's the best in the world.
If you do not feel well,
My puppy will make you feel well.

Natalie Riley (10)
Marsh Green Primary School, Wigan

Man United Football

M e and my mate playing football
A nd football makes me cool
N othing can stop me from playing football

U nited has just won three-nil
N o one is better than me
I n the middle of the pitch I saw a shin pad
T im Howard did a brilliant save
E verything about football is sporty
D ithering stood still in the net.

F ootball makes me smile
O n the top of my ball it is signed by Beckham
O ver the top of my wall is a pitch
T aught by my coach
B all in the air
A ll my friends watching me
L uck of my coin
L aughing as I scored.

C alcium from my milk
L ump from when I fell
U nited won three-nil last season
B ooster kick from my toe.

Andrew James Unsworth (10)
Marsh Green Primary School, Wigan

All The Things Found On A School Roof

A is for apple core with mould on the edge
B is for ball found on the skylight ledge
C is for car, (Jaguar I think)
D is for door handle (sprayed pink)
E is for eggshell (I wonder where that came from?)
F is for French Fries packet (eaten by Lee-Tom)
G is for gum (tutti-fruity flavour)
H is for ham (if it was fresh this I would savour),
 I is for ice-case (I'll keep that)
J is for jam jar (in the shape of a cat)
K is for kiwi fruit (messy, could be worse)
L is for lemonade log, (stuck to a purse)
M is map (Mexico circled in black!)
N is for nut (that's got a big, long crack)
O is for orange peel (eaten recently, the smell's fresh)
P is for pine cone (from Mount Cresh)
Q is for quince (I hate these)
R is for rat (urgh, oh please)
S is for strawberry (juicy and sweet)
T is for Tic-Tacs (inside smells of smelly feet!)
U is for umbrella (a segment missing off the top)
V is for bottle of Vimto (says it's sunny all week)
X is for xylophone (the tune gives a little squeak)
Y is for yacht (sprayed yellow, white and blue)
Z is for zip (from the makers of Alphabet Zoo).

And this is the alphabet of all the things found on the school roof!
Poor caretaker!

Andrew Murray (10)
Marsh Green Primary School, Wigan

Once Upon A Rhyme

A is for apple, juicy and green,
B is for banana, yellow and bent,
C is for carrot, orange and long,
D is for door, so people don't get in your house,
E is for egg, white and yellow,
F is for frog, green and jumpy,
G is for guitar, a string instrument,
H is for house, so you don't get cold,
I is for igloo, in the north pole,
J is for jokers, that make people laugh,
K is for king, who sits on the throne,
L is for lion, who lives in a zoo,
M is for mouse, people get in their house,
N is for night, when people go to sleep,
O is for orange, round and juicy,
P is for parrot, a bird in a cage,
Q is for question, someone asks,
R is for rabbits, small and cute,
S is for snake, very, very long,
T is for ten, a number,
U is for umbrella, stops you from getting wet,
V is for violin, another string instrument,
W is for Wigan, the town I live in,
X is for X-ray,
Y is for yacht, a kind of a boat,
Z is for zip.

Daryl Ravden (10)
Marsh Green Primary School, Wigan

My Rotwieller

My whining rotwieller is brown and black,
But if he's naughty I give him a smack.
When I take him for walks down the park,
He has a very loud bark.
He is very strong
And very long.
People say he runs about a metre,
But he's as fast as a cheetah.
He's very muscly on his chest,
But that's my Rotwieller, he's the best.

R otten
O ld-less
T ail
W hines
I gnorant
E ating
L oveable
L ap-sitter
E nergetic
R otwieller.

Dalton Bleakley (10)
Marsh Green Primary School, Wigan

Animal Alphabet

A is for ape, jumping around in the trees,
B is for a bird, flying away,
C is for a cat, prowling round at night,
D is for dog, running free in the park,
E is for elephant, stamping everywhere,
F is for a frog, hopping from lily to lily,
G is for a goat, running round in a meadow,
H is for a horse, eating bread and carrots,
I is for insects, walking around on six legs,
J is for a jellyfish, floating around in the ocean,
K is for a kangaroo, hopping around in the jungle,
L is for a Labrador, helping people across the road,
M is for a moth, fluttering around a light,
N is for a newt, slimy in the water,
O is for an owl, flying around at night,
P is for a python, slithering around,
Q is for quacking, just what the ducks do,
R is for a rabbit, cute as can be,
S is for a snake, scaring enemies away,
T is for a tiger, running after its prey,
U is for a unicorn, running around in dreams,
V is for a vulture, soaring around in the sky,
W is for a whale, a gigantic fish,
X is for X-ray to check the animal is not ill,
Y is for a yak, running around in a meadow,
Z is for a zebra, stripy all the time.

Rebecca Browitt (10)
Marsh Green Primary School, Wigan

Not My Clothes

Not my clothes,
mine weren't black.
Mine were white.

Not my pants,
mine weren't green.
Mine were blue,
mine had a pocket on.
Not like yours.

Not my shoes,
mine were not a pinkie colour.
Mine were black.
Not mine,
mine were Reebok
not Nike.

Not my socks,
mine weren't green.
Mine were red.
I don't like white,
I like Nike.

Now that is not my tracky-top
mine wasn't red.
Mine was multicoloured.

That's not my tie,
mine wasn't red and blue.
Mine was red, green and black!

Daniel Unsworth (10)
Marsh Green Primary School, Wigan

Once Upon A Rhyme - My Alphabet

A is for aeroplane, that is big and fast,
B is for ball, that is bouncy and small,
C is for cat, that is cuddly and fluffy,
D is for dog, that is warm and loved,
E is for elephant, that is huge and squashy,
F is for fox, that is cunning and silent,
G is for gumshield, that is protective and strong,
H is for hair, that is trendy and cool,
I is ice cream, that is yummy and runny,
J is for jelly that is wobbly and funny,
K is for kite, that goes high and low,
L is for lolly, that is sweet and tasty,
M is for Mum, who is kind and thoughtful,
N is for Nan, who is like a mum,
O is for orange, that is round and less than a pound,
P is for people, that are gentle and grateful,
Q is for queen, that cares and helps,
R is for red, that is light and bright,
S is for sport, that is amazing and enjoyable.
T is for toys, that are expensive but wicked,
U is for umbrella, that is like a shelter for everyone,
V is for vandalise, that is bad and sad,
W is for witch, who is nasty and naughty,
X is for x-ray, that tells people if things are right or wrong,
Y is for yellow, that is like the sun and a light,
Z is for zebra, that is stripy and slow.

Craig Ravden (10)
Marsh Green Primary School, Wigan

Hedgehog

The hedgehog had prickly ears,
Then he cried and shed some tears.
Then he walked away and looked this way
And in the middle of May the hedgehog had to pay.
The hedgehog had a little nose to sniff a big rose.
Then he looked at the light and it was so, so, so bright.
It was glittering like a shooting star across the sky
And the hedgehog was so cold he got told something.
The hedgehog was walking across the field
And he had a meal.
He was sitting down on the ground
And then he found a cake that the baker made.
'Yum! Yum!' he said.

Elizabeth Connolly (10)
Marsh Green Primary School, Wigan

One Windy Night

In my bed I hear the wind,
It climbs into my room,
Howling and sliding under my mum's door,
Pulling my arm to space,
Roaring at the dog,
It rattles at the windows,
But thumps down the stairs,
It dives on the chair,
Like a big man.

James Brindley (10)
Marton Primary School, Blackpool

The Moon

There the moon lays shining
In the black mass of night,
Glowing with innocence
With its companions, the stars,
Round like a ball,
Shining like the sun,
Lonely like a cloud.
When the sun's job is done
And night spreads out
The moon comes out and does its job
And shines throughout.

Bethany Butler (10)
Marton Primary School, Blackpool

Fire

I look at the fire as it burns in my eyes
As it gives off the warmth you need to survive.
A cold winter's night.
I stare and I stare and suddenly the fire spits
And I jump out like a devil.
I stare and see the angry reds and oranges
So I go to my warm, comfy bed and go to sleep.

Connor Willoughby (11)
Marton Primary School, Blackpool

The Snow

It may be dancing as it drops from the sky.
Then it whispers at the top windows.
It scatters itself all over my garden and plays
with the grass and me.
Slowly it sinks as the sun rises.
Then crawls its way to the gutter.

Ben Raby (10)
Marton Primary School, Blackpool

The Sea

I'm walking along the beach with nothing to do,
So I decide to sit down,
I can hear howls and roars,
Then I see the sea,
It's waving at me now, so I wave back,
It's as blue as the sky with white foam,
As it splashes in the air,
I now realise the time so I have to go,
So I wave at the sea and it waves back,
As I'm walking home, I realise the sea is just the sea.

Olivia Freitas (11)
Marton Primary School, Blackpool

The Snow Ballerina

The snow ballerina dances down the sky,
Twirling, whirling, pirouetting,
Sliding gracefully around the trees,
Singing with her golden voice,
Smiling at the frozen flowers below,
Skating onto the path with ease,
She whispers, 'Farewell.'

Ryan Calvert (10)
Marton Primary School, Blackpool

Angels From Above

Angels come down from Heaven
Through the soft angel-white clouds.
They like the feel of the clouds on their cheeks.
In the night when we are sleeping,
They sing their hearts aloud.
If you stay silent you may hear a quiet sound,
Whisper in your ear.

Rebecca Fletcher (10)
Marton Primary School, Blackpool

Why Oh Why Does The Fire Burn?

I'm on my own,
The fire's there burning everything,
This is a nightmare,
It's horrible, I hate it.
I want my mum,
I need my dad,
The fire's flaming,
Jumping up,
It's spitting
Help me!
I want my mum,
I need my dad,
It's burning down my house,
I want my teddy bear,
Stop! Stop! Fire!

I know you think it's funny,
To destroy people's lives
And I know you think it's funny,
That I'm talking to fire.
Well, you try being me!

Ashleigh Alladice (10)
Marton Primary School, Blackpool

Comfort

C omfort can be warm
O n my silky bed
M elted chocolate on my knee
F riends are warm and make you happy
O n a cold winter's night
R oofed under my bed
T o sleep I go.

Daniel Taylor (11)
Marton Primary School, Blackpool

The Moon

The moon shines in
The darkness of night,
Spinning around in a
Place called Nowhere.

The moon is as white
As a dull piece of paper,
Walking around in a
Place called Nowhere.

The moon looks down
At us which is the
Same as us looking
Up at him, as he floats
Around in a place called
Nowhere.

This place called
Nowhere could have
Nothing there,
But it has the moon
There as it goes
Around in this place
Called Nowhere.

Sam Purvis (11)
Marton Primary School, Blackpool

Thunder

Thunder is mean and menacing,
It roars through the night,
It charges and shouts in the evening,
Stamping down the streets,
It cries through the day,
It roars like drums,
It kills in the day and the night,
Thunder is mad, like a witch scaring
                little children in the night.

Lauren Sarah Sanderson-Roberts (11)
Marton Primary School, Blackpool

The Wind

The wind whistles
It's as cold as ice
It moves through the air
And pushes you about
The plants fall and the trees bend
We all know when the wind is around.

The wind flows
It's freezing cold.
It blows a gale
And sometimes causes a whirlwind or a hurricane.
We all know when the wind is around.

The wind is here when it snows
It's here when you're fast asleep.
It's here when you're wide awake.
The wind is here all the time
So we all know the wind is around.

Rachel Brown (11)
Marton Primary School, Blackpool

The Michael Jackson Poem

The moon walks around the Earth,
Dancing to creations of music,
Spinning, rotating around the Earth,
It covers the Round The World Tour in just a month.
It gives light at night,
To the Earth's slow move.

The moon stands out towards the stars,
It stands out more than Mercury or Mars.
It's in our system, our solar system.
It's classed as the smallest planet known.
Look through a telescope and you
Will see its amazing craters.

Joshua Alderson (10)
Marton Primary School, Blackpool

Haiku Poems

Heart
My heart has broken,
It has split into two parts.
Who will repair it?

The Sea
Enormous I am,
I wash away the dry sand,
Then I wave to you.

A City Tramp
City tramp I am,
I write questions on cardboard,
Such as: R ewe blind?

Meadow
I am a meadow,
Horses come and eat my grass,
Then they trot away.

Teddy
I am a teddy,
I am cared for but not hugged,
Suddenly I'm left.

Steven Barnes-Smith (10)
Neston Primary School, Little Neston

Baby

Attention seeker
Nappy filler
Dirty trailer
Bath splasher
Sleep stealer
Loud whiner
Squeaky squealer
House wrecker
Icky sticky
Smell maker.

Tom Lancaster (10)
Neston Primary School, Little Neston

I'm As Happy As . . .

I'm as happy as a teddy
With someone to cuddle it,
I'm as happy as the sun
With someone to praise it,
I'm as happy as a pig
With someone to feed it,
I'm as happy as a true friend
Who will never break up,
I'm as happy as a dog
Who has had a new pup,
I'm as happy as a firework
That has just gone up,
I'm as happy as a mum
Who's just found peace,
I'm as happy as me!
Can't you see!

Emily Tedford (9)
Neston Primary School, Little Neston

Monster

There's a monster in my bedroom Mum
I'll tell you what it's like
Its head is like the mountains
Its body is like wiggly worms
Its claws are like daggers
Its teeth are like cones
I know you don't believe me Mum
But hurry up because it's
Getting closer
It's . . . aarrgghh!

Corrine Abel (10)
Neston Primary School, Little Neston

The Ship

The ship is smooth
   And always moves
      The ship is rough
         When it's in a storm
            The ship is relaxing
            At the docks
               The ship is floating all the time
And the engines are as strong as a brick wall.

David Chambers (10)
Neston Primary School, Little Neston

The Monster

There's a monster in my bedroom, Mum
I'll tell you what it's like
Its head is like a massive boulder
Its body is like a wrinkly worm
Its claws are like daggers
Its teeth are like sharp mountains
I know you don't believe me, Mum
But hurry up, it's getting closer
It's . . . Argh!

Kyle Griffiths (9)
Neston Primary School, Little Neston

My World

The moon reaches out to the stars
To hold their hands like a mother cradling her baby.
Night takes its time like a hobbling old lady.
The morning wakes up the sleeping world like an opening flower.
The rain crashes down like a cold, wet shower.
The cuckoo sings sweet songs like a gospel choir.
The world stops living like a punctured flat tyre.

Faye Williams (11)
Neston Primary School, Little Neston

Mice

Wall waster
Women scarer
Cheese eater
Hole maker
Fast leaper
Food seeker
Buffet wrecker
Great hider
Amazing hearer.

Adam Harbour (10)
Neston Primary School, Little Neston

As Happy As . . .

I'm as happy as a chicken that's laid 20 eggs,
As happy as a mouse that's made a new friend,
As happy as a child at Christmas time,
As happy as a mother who's just had a baby,
As happy as a book that's just been read,
As happy as a sandwich that's been eaten,
As happy as a pig with lots of food,
As happy as a secret that somebody kept.

Daniel Green (9)
Neston Primary School, Little Neston

Football

Football is my passion
I give it my all
The real romance in my life
Is eleven men and a ball.

Dean Jones (11)
Neston Primary School, Little Neston

Monster

There's a monster in my bedroom, Mum,
I'll tell you what it's like,
Its head is like a volcano,
Its body is like a slimy snake,
Its claws are like knives,
Its teeth are like icicles,
I know you don't believe me, Mum,
But hurry up, it's getting closer,
It's . . . Argh!

Jenny Dalziel (9)
Neston Primary School, Little Neston

Monster

There's a monster in my bedroom, Mum
I'll tell you what it's like
Its head is like a haughty boulder
Its body is like slimy jelly
Its claws are like swords
Its teeth are like zigzag razors
I know you don't believe me, Mum
But hurry up, it's getting closer
It's . . . Argh!

Jason Brookes (10)
Neston Primary School, Little Neston

The Red Ferrari Haiku

The red Ferrari
Delicate and respectful
Gone in a quick flash.

Ryan Butterworth (11)
Neston Primary School, Little Neston

As Happy As . . .

I'm as happy as a bunny hopping around
As happy as a child skipping up and down
As happy as a teddy with its owner.

I'm as happy as a mum who's just had a baby
As happy as the sun shining bright
As happy as a present waiting to be opened.

I'm as happy as the sea waving to people
As happy as a boat sailing the seven seas
As happy as a firework flying around.

Natalie Williams (10)
Neston Primary School, Little Neston

Dancer

Bum shaker
Rhythm mover
Back flipper
Foot braker
Dance partner
Belly flopper
Good mover
Attention seeker.

Ashley White (10)
Neston Primary School, Little Neston

Who Is She?

I feel as tall as a towering skyscraper.
I feel as small as a ladybird.
She seems as frightening as a bear.
I know I'm shaking like jelly on a plate.
She seems to roar like a lion.
I sound as quiet as a baby asleep.
But I hope she's really as gentle as a teddy bear.
Because sometimes I behave like a chimpanzee.
Who is she?
She's my new teacher.

Amy Hill (10)
Neston Primary School, Little Neston

Dogs

Meat eater
Bed finder
Dirty drooler
Furniture trailer
Loud howler
Skin waster
Flea seeker
House wrecker
Rubbish actor.

Tom Wilcock (10)
Neston Primary School, Little Neston

My Star

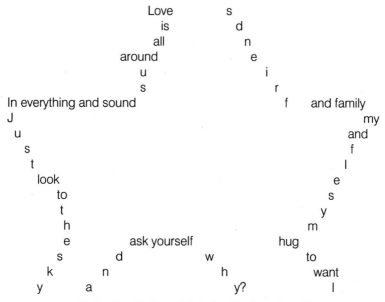

```
        Love        s
         is         d
         all         n
       around         e
          u            i
          s             r
In everything and sound    f    and family
J                                         my
 u                                        and
  s                                         f
   t                                        l
    look                                   e
      to                                  s
      t                                  y
     h                                m
    e         ask yourself        hug
   s       d            w          to
  k      n            h           want
 y     a            y?             l
```

Rebecca McKay (8) & Joelle Cavalot (9)
Our Lady Of The Assumption RC Primary School, Blackpool

Untitled

Once upon a rhyme
There was a panda
He lived in a forest
And he fell into the pond.

And he swam to China
He went to the China café to get a drink
But they wouldn't let him in.

Then he cried
And then he saw his mum
And his mum gave him a big hug
And they lived happily ever after.

Ryan Chapman (9)
Our Lady Of The Assumption RC Primary School, Blackpool

The Dark, Dark House!

Once upon a rhyme,
There was a *dark, dark* house!
And in the *dark, dark* house, there
Was a *crash*
    bang
    boom
The dog and the cat

In the *dark, dark* room
There was a *crash*
    bang
    boom
    ding
    dong
The mouse, cat and the dog

In the *dark, dark* box
was a *crash*
    bang
    boom
    ding
    dong
    bling
The mouse, cat, dog and the man

In the *dark, dark* shoe
was a *crash*
    bang
    boom
    ding
    dong
    bling
    yo
The mouse, cat, dog, man and
Monster!

Alexander Williams & Curtis Clough (8)
Our Lady Of The Assumption RC Primary School, Blackpool

Once Upon A Time . . .

Once upon a time, I had a friend
But we broke up
But a cat came in
We don't know how
For some strange reason
It makes us friends

So then we played football
It was so much fun
I scored a goal
And my friend scored one.

Then we played with some toys
We had a battle with some army toys
We both drew.
Then we went out to get our bikes
We had a race on our bikes.
Then Josh won, and Josh had to go in to have his dinner.

Macauley Rogerson (8)
Our Lady Of The Assumption RC Primary School, Blackpool

Ice Skating

I ce
C arefully
E xcited

S creeching
K icking ice
A nswering ice questions
T wisting
I ce cubes
N ets
G rind.

Andrew Lonican (8)
Our Lady Of The Assumption RC Primary School, Blackpool

Dreams

I dream about some wonderful things,
Or scary things like a ghost that goes *boo!*
I dream about a small bird that sings,
Ring, ring, the alarm, noooo!

I'm back to sleep,
What will I dream?
Maybe a car horn that goes, *peep, peep!*
Or the girls' netball team.
Morning time already?

Hannah Smith (9)
Our Lady Of The Assumption RC Primary School, Blackpool

My Car

My car has a crazy design
My car has lots of space
My car has a CD player
My car has a smiling face.

My car has a huge engine
My car goes like the wind
My car has a little draught
My car has never spinned!

Daniel Moss (9)
Our Lady Of The Assumption RC Primary School, Blackpool

Untitled

In a dark, dark forest
    There was a dark, dark house
        In the dark, dark house there was a dark, dark room

In the dark, dark room there was a dark, creepy floor and when
    you step on it, it goes . . .
        Eeeeeeeeeee!

Jacob Lawton-Jones (8)
Our Lady Of The Assumption RC Primary School, Blackpool

Untitled

I rode my car
With my friend John.
We fell off it
And landed in a well.

Then we got back up
We were wet and soggy
It didn't matter
Because it was foggy!

Connor Jordan (9)
Our Lady Of The Assumption RC Primary School, Blackpool

Death

Death killed,
We were separated.
Love was murdered,
Death is darkness.

Death destroyed my heart,
Tore my emotions.
Ruined my mind
Left me lonely.

Emily Kiggin (11)
Plodder Lane CP School, Farnworth

The Rainbow

The rainbow makes a colourful sky,
A pot of gold, full of promise.
The rainbow is magical,
Granting wishes for people.

John McAtee (11)
Plodder Lane CP School, Farnworth

The Eruption

Smoke roars through the sky
Children and adults
Smothering their cry
Fear of a slow and painful death
Burned, burned in the eruption.

The colour of lava
Red and yellow,
Smoky sky and
Steaming ground,
Lava jumps to touch the sky
Burned, burned in the eruption.

The volcano is a warrior.
Long live the volcano!

Sarah Taylor (10)
Plodder Lane CP School, Farnworth

The Eruption

The dragon awakes from his slumber,
Lashing out his sleepy tail,
Making the mountain shudder,
Giving out a furious roar.

The dragon rests now,
The city covered with ash forever,
Back to slumbering now, he's dormant
Till next time when he awakes.

James Howe (10)
Plodder Lane CP School, Farnworth

Fear

Fear picked at my brain,
Sat on my heart,
Drove me insane,
Fear conquered my soul.

Fear told me to ignore my senses,
Dictated my actions,
Controlled my speech,
Stole my time.

Fear, my foe,
My ancient enemy.

Heather McGill (10)
Plodder Lane CP School, Farnworth

The Volcano

The monster awakes,
Shakes off his sleep,
Ash suffocates the town,
A cloud of dust and gas,
Roams the sky.

A river of lava
Melts and destroys
All in its path.
It's like a giant firework display
But not in November.

Andrew Barber (11)
Plodder Lane CP School, Farnworth

Volcano

The volcano is in red,
It sleeps in his bed,
Roaring and rolling around.
Through night and day
It mumbles away,
Making a terrible sound.

Then it starts to scream;
It's gone from nice to mean.
It's angry and ready to blow.
So run away
To a place where it can never go.

Jade Hodges (11)
Plodder Lane CP School, Farnworth

The Storm

The wind is a wild wolf.
The thunder,
It's howling at the moon.
An electric flash!
Then his saliva drips over the world.
He tires,
Returns to his home:
A cloudy kennel in the sky.
Chased by the wind,
He is followed by a jewelled sky.

Alex Barker (10)
Plodder Lane CP School, Farnworth

The Eruption

The eruption is a thunderous giant.
Who shatters the blue sky.
He roars like a lion,
Spitting ash through the broken sapphire.
He sends a river of lava
To the terrified people,
Showing his ugly fury
As he spurts his top off
Crushing the people with his arms.

Greg Wright (10)
Plodder Lane CP School, Farnworth

What Is The Weather?

Why does it thunder?
Because the gods are clashing down.
What is rain?
A tree's sorrow to be cut down.
Why is it windy?
A giant is sneezing down.
Why does it snow?
Because the clouds are falling apart.
Why is the sun hot?
It's God's cigarette tip.

Jackson Casson (10)
Primrose Hill Primary School, Euxton

Man U

Man U,
After the match,
The last of the season,
And The Premiership trophy
Is ours!

Rhiannon Lucas (11)
Primrose Hill Primary School, Euxton

Lightning

Lights up the sky
Causes people to die.

A bright flash
A godly clash.

Makes trees fall
However tall.

Happens in rain
Could destroy a crane.

Interferes with TVs
Doesn't please bees.

Shatters roofs
Shakes horses' hooves.

It is brightening
It is lightning.

Connor Miles (10)
Primrose Hill Primary School, Euxton

Weather

What is thunder?
God's rage and anger.

What is the sun?
A fire orange.

What is the rain?
God's tap on in the bathroom.

What is fog?
God having a BBQ.

Thomas Bowker (11)
Primrose Hill Primary School, Euxton

Cinquains

The goal
The ball
Kicked by a boy
What a fabulous shot
It slipped past the goalkeeper's hands . . .
A goal!

Wicked
Wake up!
It's Christmas Day
We all ran down the stairs
We tore off the wrapping paper . . .
Wicked . . .

Mark Chapman
Primrose Hill Primary School, Euxton

Kennings

A round ball,
Something small,

A cracking shell,
It broke well,

A scaly skin,
A rough chin,

A smooth crawler,
A death roller,

A good killer,
A mouth filler.

Sam Parker (11)
Primrose Hill Primary School, Euxton

What Is The Weather?

Why does it rain?
It's the giants crying.

Why does it snow?
It's the clouds doing a spot of dusting.

What is fog?
The ghost of Heaven welcoming someone when they die.

Why does the rainbow have so many colours?
It's God's smile in many different moods.

What is thunder?
Wild horses galloping through the grey heavens.

What is a tornado?
It's God sneezing.

What is a whirlpool?
Dead people from an old sunken ship,
being sucked into the depths of Hell.

What is lightning?
It's the sun talking to the moon.

How is fire started?
It's the burning embers of dead animals.

Who is God?
. . . I don't know.

Sally Nuttall (10)
Primrose Hill Primary School, Euxton

Thank You!

Dear Aunty,
 The make-up was simply amazing,
 Who told you what to choose?
 Because it was black and white,
 It goes great with my shiny shoes.

Dear Gran,
 The Barbie pyjamas were cool,
 You got the idea from my mother.
 I hope they will last forever,
 Because they go great with my Sindy bed cover.

Dear Uncle,
 Thanks for the shampoo, it's great,
 It makes my hair smell of cherry.
 How did you know I'd run out,
 Of last year's shampoo - strawberry?

Ashleigh Branston (11)
Primrose Hill Primary School, Euxton

Get Up Cinquain

'Get up!'
Mum yelled upstairs
I fell out of my bed
With the shock of my mum's loud voice
I groaned.

Thomas McIlroy
Primrose Hill Primary School, Euxton

What Is The Weather?

What's the sun?
Giants having a bonfire.
Why does it thunder?
Gods are on their pogo sticks.
What is hail?
Unicorns kicking stones.
Why does it rain?
Clouds are crying down.
Why does it snow?
Sheep are being sheared.
Why does it get cold?
The sun spends most of its time in Australia!

Dan Hull (11)
Primrose Hill Primary School, Euxton

Limerick

There was an old man of noo noo
Who stood in a pile of dog poo
He felt very dim
They all laughed at him
That poor little man of noo noo.

There was a young boy from China
Who was a real bad whiner
Mum gave him a clout
And she kicked him out
That poor little boy from China.

James Thompson (10)
Primrose Hill Primary School, Euxton

Sea Poem

I must go down to the shore again
To see the waves splash and the shells
And all I ask is a calm sea
With the wind, the rain and the rocks
I'd love to see a pirate ship
And a captain to steer it by
But most of all a ship's crew
And a white sail stuck up high
Angry in despair.

Timmy Parker (9)
Romiley Primary School, Romiley

Down Beneath The Ocean

Down beneath the ocean, one hundred metres deep,
Lie the mermaids and their friends quietly fast asleep,
At daybreak eyes like diamonds shall open among the seas,
I'd like to be a mermaid and ring the bells of peace,
Swimming round in circles, just look at the mermaids go,
Ever crashing waves, doesn't the beauty show.

Gemma Lewis (8)
Romiley Primary School, Romiley

The Sea

Slowly the light fades away,
Slowly the rocks crumble,
Slowly the birds fly away,
Slowly the fish glide through the sea,
Slowly the fishermen carry their nets off,
Slowly the tide sucks the shore.

Oliver Norman (9)
Romiley Primary School, Romiley

Fish Swim

Fish swim
Crabs crawl
Sea snakes slither
Eels wiggle around
Starfish grip on rocks
People dive
Seals play
Dolphins jump
That's what happens in the ocean.

Ella Osiyemi (8)
Romiley Primary School, Romiley

Pets

Pets are here,
Pets are there,
Pets, oh pets are everywhere.
I love pets,
I do care,
I love my pet that's everywhere.

Harley Duffy (8)
Romiley Primary School, Romiley

Slowly

Slowly the snow falls from the sky,
Slowly the foxes come out in the long, dark night,
Slowly the night falls on the forest,
Slowly the hands move round the clock,
Slowly the old man mounts the style,
Slowly the cat's eyes start to *glow!*

Jessica Woolridge (9)
Romiley Primary School, Romiley

Benjamin And Molly Rabbit

Benjamin Rabbit likes to play and run,
Before you know it he's gone like a gun.
He's whiter than snow and faster than a cat,
His sister Molly Rabbit is getting quite fat.

Molly is brown and hides in the mud,
But Benjamin soon finds her, his eyesight is good.
Benjamin protects Molly because she is small,
Their mum and dad are at the vet's, they had a bad fall.

Benjamin likes carrots and Molly likes straw,
After they've had some, they sit there for more!
At 9 o'clock it's time for bed,
Benjamin and Molly have another long day ahead.

Eleanor Gilbert (9)
Romiley Primary School, Romiley

I Wonder What Becomes . . .

I wonder what becomes of the seaside
When all the children have left
When grown-ups have gone
No ice creams
No lemonade
No buckets
No spades
Not even a lonely man walking upon the shore
A dog barking in the distance
No, not that I can hear
Nothing, no nothing at all.

Amie Meadows (9)
Romiley Primary School, Romiley

Winter's Coming

Winter's coming
Cold and silent

Snowflakes falling
To cover the land

Fields of white
Sheets of snow

Robins hopping
To and fro

Cowbells ringing
Ring, ring, ring

Ducks quacking
On the icy pond

Out comes the sun
To melt the snow.

Sam Fazackerley (8)
Romiley Primary School, Romiley

Caravan

I must go down to the caravan again;
To feed the horse and the cows
All I ask is saddles and reins
And people to walk her by
And the horse's song and the
Cows' *moos* and my friends listening.
I must go down to the caravan again;
To go play with my friends
To hear the tractor
To see my grandma
And to feel the lonely sheep.

Grace Donovan (8)
Romiley Primary School, Romiley

The Sea

The sea has fish of all different kinds,
The sea has many different minds.

The sand, the caves, the soft blue waves
And the sea holds slaves of boats and caves.

On a stormy night a flash of light would hit the pier
When the old man's children are still here.

The wall would fall and the sea would crawl,
Onto the paths and drench them all.

The spume would fly and hit the ground
And it just makes such a deafening sound
And then the sea would flow into a band
And go back to the golden sand.

Ben Jones (9)
Romiley Primary School, Romiley

Winter Comes

Winter comes
With the sound of the beautiful robin singing in the trees
Winter comes
When there is no sight of bees
Winter comes
When snowflakes fall from the sky
Winter comes
When I can smell the scent of apple pie
Winter comes
When it feels cold outside
Winter comes
When all the fields turn white.

Eva Morewood (8)
Romiley Primary School, Romiley

A Roller Coaster Ride

The ride starts rolling
The speed gets faster and faster
Like a racing car driver
It twists and turns on the bumpy track
It whizzes and whooshes through the sky
It skids and swerves
It's going down and down
Like a swooping owl
I'm going to dive
Like Jonny Wilkinson scoring a try
It's getting slower and slower
Suddenly,
Stop!

James Prike (9)
Romiley Primary School, Romiley

Cold

Cold fingers,
Cold toes,
Pink sky,
Pink nose.

Birds whistle,
Branches crack,
Home again,
Winter's back.

Roads freeze,
Sun red,
Warm room,
Warm bed.

Jasmine Crone (8)
Romiley Primary School, Romiley

Winter

Winter comes with snowflakes falling,
Winter comes with children running,
Winter comes with teachers shouting,
Winter comes with snowballs flying,
Winter comes with wellies stomping,
Winter comes with lakes a-freezing,
Winter comes with hedgehogs sleeping,
Winter comes with children shouting,
Winter comes with grown-ups shopping,
Winter comes with Santa flying,
Winter comes with sleigh bells ringing,
Winter comes with snowmen standing,
Winter comes with babies crying,
Winter comes with children laughing,
Winter comes no matter what.

Paige Wilkinson (9)
Romiley Primary School, Romiley

The Fields

I must go down to the fields again,
To watch the drifting snow.

I must go down to the fields again,
To help the plants grow.

Even though the weather is cold,
I must find the treasure it holds.

I must go down to the fields again,
To watch the drifting snow settle.

Emily Schofield (9)
Romiley Primary School, Romiley

Bathing

Sitting on my lilo,
Swishing my feet in the water,
The little fish tickling my feet,
As they swim past in the cool water.

The sea as still as a waiting fox,
Ready to strike on a rabbit,
The lilo is the colour of the setting sun,
As tidy as a ready-made chair.

I sit there on my lilo,
Thinking of wonderful fantasies,
The lilo starts to drift away,
In happy thought like me.

I can't wait till tomorrow I think
Before I fall off to sleep.

Naomi S Pollitt (8)
Romiley Primary School, Romiley

The Sea

Sand's still
Waves splash
Fish swim
Sharks eat
Scales sparkle
Children play
People bathe
Boats float
Schools swim
Anemones still
Mysteries secret
Treasure shines.

Morgan Reilly (9)
Romiley Primary School, Romiley

Beach Fever

I must go down to the beach again,
To the seagulls soaring high
And all I ask is a rowing boat
And navigation to steer me by.

I must go down to the beach again,
To the cool sea and sand
I really want a tidal wave
And some lifeboats to be manned.

I must go down to the beach again,
With all the waves crashing,
Whales moaning, sharks gnashing
And a lighthouse light flashing.

Verity Young (9)
Romiley Primary School, Romiley

I Must Go Down To The Beach Again

I must go down to the beach again,
To see the waves roaring gently.

I must go down to the beach again,
To see the boats bobbing up and down.

I must go down to the beach again,
To see all my friends.

I must go down to the beach again,
To see the tide creeping right behind me.

Leah Heath (9)
Romiley Primary School, Romiley

At The Sea

I want a ship
To have a dip
In the great Pacific Ocean.

I want a ship
To have a dip
And swim away with the whales.

I want a ship
To have a dip
And see the rolling tides.

At the end of the day
I'll shout, 'Wey-hey!'
And everyone will hear me.

Joel Patchett (9)
Romiley Primary School, Romiley

Snow

Snowflakes fall,
I make a snowball.

Snow turns to ice,
I think it's nice.

Snow stops falling,
We start snowballing.

I make a snowman,
I say, 'Hello Man.'

Sky is white,
It's nearly night.

Emily Blackshaw (8)
Romiley Primary School, Romiley

The Wailing Sea

The wailing sea howling,
The sky darkened with people running.

The wailing sea has its powers,
Whales and dolphins swimming.

Sharks finding their prey for fish
The wailing sea is coming in.

The tide has come
It's time to go.

But the wailing sea
Will be back another day,
So watch out!

Jack Barraclough (9)
Romiley Primary School, Romiley

Sea And Sand Time

The sea is loud,
The sand is quiet,
The sea roars,
The sand blows in the wind.

The bright blue sea is sharp,
The solemn sand always shivers.

The starfish lies on the shore,
The white horses rush about,
But while the sand and the sea
Do their job I lie happily on the rocks
While the sun sets.

Georgia Lawrie (9)
Romiley Primary School, Romiley

Snow Is Falling

Snow is falling,
Frost-bitten fingers
Snowballs flying
Hitting people
In the leg.

Building walls
Castles
Bridges
Lots of snowflakes
Snowmen getting built
Sky is grey
It's the end of day.

Daniel Hawes (8)
Romiley Primary School, Romiley

What If . . . ?

What if a snake could talk?
What if a monkey used forks?

What if fish could fly?
What if crocodiles could cry?

What if dogs could rhyme?
What if rats could climb?

What if lions could punch?
What if elephants could pack their lunch?

What if tigers could sing?
What if bears could sting?

Bethan Hurdsfield (8)
Romiley Primary School, Romiley

My Dog

My dog bites other dogs
And he hunts
He crawls around and barks
He's white and brown
He's round and straight
His fur is thick
He's loud and has low barks
He's small and fat
My dog is the best dog in the whole wide world.

Carl Cunliffe
St John's RC Primary School, Bromley Cross

Pippin The Dog

I see a dog curled up as a cushion
I see a dog jumping low
I see a dog golden and fluffy
I see a dog as kind as a person
I see a dog, soft
I see a dog barking loudly
I see a dog sleeping quietly
I see a dog as my friend.

Nicholas Bannister (9)
St John's RC Primary School, Bromley Cross

I See A Cat

I see a cat sleeping
I see a cat walking slowly
I see a cat miaowing at night
While everybody is in bed
I see a cat eating food
It slowly walks across the room
I see a cat
Its colour is black.

Luke Bradbury (9)
St John's RC Primary School, Bromley Cross

My Cat

I see a cat . . .
with gleaming green eyes and a pink nose
pointy whiskers, sharp claws.
Its colour is a ginger, black and brown mix.
Short, smooth and soft fur.
Playing with a ball of tin foil,
moving quickly, pouncing frantically.
Purrs quietly, miaows noisily,
stalking hungrily, glaring meanly,
freezes and prepares to pounce.

Kate Howarth (8)
St John's RC Primary School, Bromley Cross

I See A Duck

I see a duck
as bright as the sun.
I see a duck
flying, jumping and swimming.
His beak as sharp as a pin
feathers glistening in the sunlight.
They feel smooth, silky and furry
I wish I was a duck.

Matthew Hunt (9)
St John's RC Primary School, Bromley Cross

I Saw A Dolphin

I saw a dolphin swimming through the sea.
It was moving slowly and silently.
It had smooth, soft skin.
It was grey.
Sometimes it made squeaking noises
But most of the time it just swam around
In the sea.

Chania Williams (9)
St John's RC Primary School, Bromley Cross

That Is The Dolphin I Saw

I see a dolphin
      splashing and leaping around
flicking its tail
      with light grey and dark blue skin.
Its body is like a wave
      very smooth skin
it goes *ark, ark, ark.*
      It swims under water
that is the dolphin I saw.

Louise Latham (8)
St John's RC Primary School, Bromley Cross

I See A Fish

I see a fish
swimming joyfully
moving swiftly
brown and green colours all over.
As thin as paper
soft and scaly
bubbles and splashes,
that's my fish.

Matthew Deegan (8)
St John's RC Primary School, Bromley Cross

I See A Dog

I see a dog
Who is sleeping on the floor
I see him barking at the milkman
Running and running round the tree
Catching the little bird for his tea
That's my dog
My sweet dog.

Charlotte Brooks (8)
St John's RC Primary School, Bromley Cross

I See A Snake

It's slithering silently
It moves very sneakily
It is green and grey
It's long and scaly
Its skin is rough and slimy
It hisses and bites
Spitting poison at enemies
I see a snake.

Callum Short (8)
St John's RC Primary School, Bromley Cross

A Dolphin

I see a dolphin
Swimming, jumping into the air
Then side to side it goes
It's as grey as the clouds
Its skin is like smooth rubber
It squawks like a bird
It does tricks like they do in a circus
Suddenly it's gone.

Isobel Keating (8)
St John's RC Primary School, Bromley Cross

I Have A Cheetah In Me

I have a cheetah in me
Hunting in the night
As fast as lightning
As yellow as the sun with brown spots
As fierce as a gladiator
Its fur's like a lion's skin.

Nathan Rothwell (8)
St John's RC Primary School, Bromley Cross

My Kangaroo

I see a kangaroo
jumping high
hopping wildly
running in water
running like thunder.
It is quite thin and small
its fur is very soft and cuddly
it doesn't make a sound
it is very quiet
it is very careful with its baby
it plays with its baby
it jumps
it tries every day to catch a mouse
but they're too fast.
He is a silly kangaroo
and very playful.

Patrick Jarvis (9)
St John's RC Primary School, Bromley Cross

I See A Fish

I see a fish . . .
Swimming in the tank
He looks out
Splashing in the water
Gliding through the tunnel
His shiny orange scales are very bright
He is a greedy fish
He jumps out of the water for food
He does not make a noise but blows bubbles
He picks up stones and drops them
Thomas is my silent pet.

Michael Ball (9)
St John's RC Primary School, Bromley Cross

My Hamster

Running in a space ball,
Moving like an orang-utan,
Black as night,
White as snow,
Is the colour of my animal.
It's as smooth as a rabbit,
A scratching sound like a cat on a post,
It sleeps through the day,
That's a hamster,
My hamster.

Rachel Antrobus (9)
St John's RC Primary School, Bromley Cross

I See A Puppy

I see a puppy
A very angry puppy
Running very fast
Bending his legs.
His body shape is sort of rectangular
His fur is soft and hairy
He eats dog food,
All different flavours.
This is the puppy I see.

Daniel McQuaid (9)
St John's RC Primary School, Bromley Cross

My Cat

I see a cat . . .
Jumping and leaping,
Sneaking and creeping,
As grey as a cloud,
As white as snow,
As long as a sausage,
As soft as felt.
It will rub against your leg,
It will purr when you stroke it,
It will go to sleep on your lap.

Megan Walsh (8)
St John's RC Primary School, Bromley Cross

I See A Tiger

It is sneaking up on its prey
It is running most of the time
It has blue eyes
Its skin is like velvet
It's a loud growler
It's a good jumper,
Good for catching its prey
And when it kills its prey
It eats proudly.
When you see a tiger,
Run away.

Alex King (8)
St John's RC Primary School, Bromley Cross

Molly

I see a small, furry dog called Molly
that is doing a roly-poly in the mud
and moving very quickly.
Its fur is smooth and soft
its multicoloured fur is clean and sparkly
with some patches as white as snow
others as black as ink
and one as brown as golden hair.

Jack Corrigan (9)
St John's RC Primary School, Bromley Cross

The Writer Of This Poem

(Based on 'The Writer Of This Poem' by Roger McGough)

The writer of this poem . . .
Is as good-looking as can be
As bold as a full stop
As busy as a bee
As clean as cotton wool
As strong as an ox
As fast as the wind
As sly as a fox
As tall as a giraffe
As wild as a boar
As big as an elephant
As wide as a door
The writer of this poem
Likes to read 'Green Eggs and Ham'
Which is a book by Dr Seuss
And my name is Sam.

Samuel Gormally (9)
St Mary's Birchley RC Primary School, Billinge

Beyond The Door

(Based on 'The Door' by Miroslav Holub)

Go and open the door
Maybe outside there's
A giant beanstalk
Or a leaping frog
Or there's a spooky,
Haunted house.

Go and open the door
Maybe there's a magic dinosaur
Maybe there's a golden ribbon
Or a famous lily
Or a flying dog.

Go and open the door
If there's nothing there
At least there'll be a draught.

Stephen Wiles (8)
St Mary's Birchley RC Primary School, Billinge

Beyond The Door

(Based on 'The Door' by Miroslav Holub)

Go and open the door
Maybe outside there's a giant beanstalk
With a giant at the top or a spooky ghost.

Go and open the door
Maybe there's a leaping frog
Maybe there's a magical magician
Or a golden ring
Or a flying cat.

Go and open the door
If you see a monster it will be alright
Just go and open the door.

Liam Baines (7)
St Mary's Birchley RC Primary School, Billinge

The Writer Of This Poem

(Based on 'The Writer Of This Poem' by Roger McGough)

The writer of this poem
Is as tall as a tree
As fast as the wind
As busy as a bee
As messy as a fuzzy bear
As fun as a cat
As wise as an old owl
As soft as a mat
As shiny as a sunbeam
As bright as stripy socks
As sharp as a staple
As flexible as a box
The writer of this poem
Is as fun as can be
Her name is Natalie Bannister
And that is me!

Natalie Bannister (10)
St Mary's Birchley RC Primary School, Billinge

Beyond The Door

(Based on 'The Door' by Miroslav Holub)

Go and open the door
Maybe outside there is
A hollow tree,
Maybe there are people,
Or a rainforest.

Go and open the door,
Maybe there is a golden city,
Maybe there is a jungle,
Or a dark land,
Or a wonderland.

Go and open the door,
If you do you will be cursed,
It will haunt you . . .

Thomas Harrison (7)
St Mary's Birchley RC Primary School, Billinge

The Writer Of This Poem

(Based on 'The Writer Of This Poem' by Roger McGough)

The writer of this poem . . .
Is as small as a mouse
As funny as a toad
As strong as a house
As nice as a hamster
As old as a tree
As thin as a stick
As happy as you and me
As clever as a computer
As light as a feather
As floaty as a cloud
As soft as leather
The writer of this poem . . .
Can jump more than a metre
He's as cheeky as a monkey
And his name is Peter.

Peter Bostock (9)
St Mary's Birchley RC Primary School, Billinge

Dreaming Is Like . . .

Dreaming is like your favourite movie
Dreaming is like drinking smoothies
Dreaming is like flying high
Dreaming is like a life without a sigh
Dreaming is like a pool of water
Dreaming is like a life without slaughter.

Bob Keegan (8)
St Mary's Birchley RC Primary School, Billinge

Beyond The Door
(Based on 'The Door' by Miroslav Holub)

Go and open the door.
Maybe outside there's
a magic castle,
a fairground, a forest
or paradise.

Go and open the door.
Maybe a secret garden
maybe a gold house
or a rainforest
or an old city.

Go and open the door.
If you do
it will grant you three wishes.

Harriet Collinson (8)
St Mary's Birchley RC Primary School, Billinge

Dreaming Is Like . . .

Dreaming is like going on an adventure that never ends,
Dreaming is like diving into a pool with velvet waves,
Dreaming is like sailing in a boat on a never-ending sea,
Dreaming is like getting in bed and never waking up,
Dreaming is like swimming in a pool of chocolate sauce,
Dreaming is like winning a never-ending race,
Dreaming is like going to the moon and never coming back.

Ellen Gravener (8)
St Mary's Birchley RC Primary School, Billinge

Tiger Haiku

In a deep jungle
Walks a colourful tiger
Like a tabby cat.

Louise Riley (10)
St Mary's Birchley RC Primary School, Billinge

Beyond The Door

(Based on 'The Door' by Miroslav Holub)

Go and open the door
Maybe outside there's a dog giving birth
Or a dragon
Or a big heap of earth.

Go and open the door
Maybe there's a secret garden
Maybe there's a castle
Or a dancing monkey
Or a bunny with her friends.

Go and open the door
If there's only a wind
It will be nice and cool
At least there'll be some sun.

Rosanna Owen (8)
St Mary's Birchley RC Primary School, Billinge

In A Moment Of Silence

In a moment of silence on the moor I could hear
the brilliant birds twittering their tune

In a moment of silence in the jungle I could hear
an enormous elephant stomping its way along

In a moment of silence at the North Pole I could hear
gigantic growls from a picture perfect polar bear

In a moment of silence in Egypt I could hear
the Egyptian vultures squawking above my head.

Archie McCluskey (8)
St Mary's Birchley RC Primary School, Billinge

The Writer Of This Poem

(Based on 'The Writer Of This Poem' by Roger McGough)

The writer of this poem . . .
Is as small as a mouse
As pretty as a princess
As strong as a house
As wise as an owl
As thin as a pin
As soft as a baby's bum
As hard as a tin
As bright as the sun
As busy as a bee
As clean as tap water
As cute as can be
The writer of this poem
Is as deep as a hole
The writer of this poem
Is called Nicole.

Nicole Friar (9)
St Mary's Birchley RC Primary School, Billinge

Inside My Marble

I can see the world inside out and upside down,
I can see chocolate ice cream mountains with strawberry sauce,
I can see dogs and cats eating sweets,
I can see horses learning and playing on computers,
I can see houses made from sweets and chocolate,
I can see me and my family in a palace of money,
I can see an elephant shaking hands with an ant,
I would love to go inside my marble would you?

Alysha Burrows (8)
St Mary's Birchley RC Primary School, Billinge

The Writer Of This Poem

(Based on 'The Writer Of This Poem' by Roger McGough)

The writer of this poem . . .
Is as clever as an owl
As big as a house
As fierce as a lion's growl
As fast as a shark
As bendy as a spoon
As smelly as socks
As bright as the moon
As good as gold
As friendly as a sunbeam
As strong as concrete
As smooth as cream
The writer of this poem . . .
Likes to scream and rant
He has an awful temper
And his name is Grant.

Grant Oldham (10)
St Mary's Birchley RC Primary School, Billinge

Mum Kenning

Bedroom cleaner
Bedtime dreamer

Kitchen sweeper
Night-time creeper

Busy shopper
Night mopper

Husband lover
My mother.

Samantha Morrisby (10)
St Mary's Birchley RC Primary School, Billinge

The Writer Of This Poem

(Based on 'The Writer Of This Poem' by Roger McGough)

The writer of this poem . . .
Is as fast as a car
As cute as a puppy
As bright as a star
As clean as a pig
As sweet as a lolly
As bad as a baby
As prickly as holly
As thin as a flower
As nice as you
As scary as a bat
As loud as *boo!*
The writer of this poem . . .
Is like a bee being busy
The writer of this poem
Is a girl called Lizzy.

Elizabeth Logan (10)
St Mary's Birchley RC Primary School, Billinge

Beyond The Door

(Based on 'The Door' by Miroslav Holub)

Go and open the door.
Maybe outside there's a grasshopper
an ant or a forest.

Go and open the door.
Maybe a cat is sleeping
maybe a frog is leaping
or maybe there is a dinosaur
or a spooky castle.

Go and open the door.
If there is rain
it will dry.

Elizabeth Bannister (8)
St Mary's Birchley RC Primary School, Billinge

The Writer Of This Poem

(Based on 'The Writer Of This Poem' by Roger McGough)

The writer of this poem . . .
Is stronger than a brick
As flexible as paper
As tall as a long stick
As sharp as a fang
As cute as can be
As clever as anything
As small as a flea
As sticky as Sellotape
As sweet as a cat
As wobbly as jelly
As flat as a mat
The writer of this poem . . .
Likes to play football
He is a boy called Robert Foster
And he knows it all.

Robert Foster (9)
St Mary's Birchley RC Primary School, Billinge

Haikus And Cinquains

Haiku
The little red fox
Prowls in the dark alleyway
Looking for some food.

Cinquain
Raining
It makes puddles
On the wet and damp ground
It comes from the black misty sky
Dripping.

Beth Frackelton (10)
St Mary's Birchley RC Primary School, Billinge

The Writer Of This Poem

(Based on 'The Writer Of This Poem' by Roger McGough)

The writer of this poem . . .
Is as beautiful as can be
As smart as a teacher
As tall as a tree
As skinny as a pencil
As bright as the sun
As red as a rose
As tasty as a bun
As strong as a boulder
As cheeky as a monkey
As brainy as a laptop
As cool as funky
The writer of this poem . . .
Is as fun as can be
Flies as high as a bird
Of course it's me!

Hannah Quirk (9)
St Mary's Birchley RC Primary School, Billinge

I Want To Paint

I want to paint happy feelings
I want to paint orange peeling
I want to paint the taste of curry
I want to paint someone in a hurry
I want to paint the taste of cake
I want to paint a duck in a lake.

Laurie-Jane Wilson (9)
St Mary's Birchley RC Primary School, Billinge

The Writer Of This Poem

(Based on 'The Writer Of This Poem' by Roger McGough)

The writer of this poem . . .
Is smaller than a bin
As wise as an owl
As pale as some skin
As dopey as a crow
As bright as a tick
As smart as a teacher
As thick as a brick
As quick as a cheetah
As sharp as lead
As straight as a ruler
As steady as a bed
The writer of this poem
Is as busy as a bee
The writer of this poem
Is obviously me!

George Collinson (9)
St Mary's Birchley RC Primary School, Billinge

Inside My Marble

I can see me holding the trophy for England,
I can see me driving a F1 racing car,
I can see Liverpool beating Man United at Anfield,
I can see Pluto five times bigger than the sun.
I can see the moon floating closer to Earth,
I can see all the dinosaurs flying to Earth,
I would love to go inside my marble
Would you?

Michael Mellor (8)
St Mary's Birchley RC Primary School, Billinge

The Writer Of This Poem

(Based on 'The Writer Of This Poem' by Roger McGough)

The writer of this poem . . .
Is as smart as can be
As strong as a boxer
As hard as a tree
As thin as an earthworm
As handsome as a king
As nice as a fluffy dog
As sparkly as a ring
As fast as a cheetah
As cool as a frozen pool
As sharp as a pin
As thick as a fool
The writer of this poem
Is a sturdy as a brick
The writer of this poem is
Called Matthew Frederick.

Matthew Frederick (10)
St Mary's Birchley RC Primary School, Billinge

Inside My Marble

Inside my marble, I can see the red lava
pouring out of a rock solid volcano.

Inside my marble, I can see a magical world
rolling upon the moon.

Inside my marble, I can see a million football pitches
all over the world.

Inside my marble, I can see me helping Michael Owen
play fab football on the football pitch.

Thomas Spencer (9)
St Mary's Birchley RC Primary School, Billinge

Cinquain

Snowing
Cold and frosty
Snow falls from the grey sky
Children play and make fat snowmen.

Beth Howard (10)
St Mary's Birchley RC Primary School, Billinge

In The Forest Haiku

In the forest green
The spiky little hedgehog
Like a crawling mouse.

Jennifer Keane (10)
St Mary's Birchley RC Primary School, Billinge

Butterfly Haiku

In my back garden
Floats a gentle butterfly
Moving silently.

Elizabeth Hague (11)
St Mary's Birchley RC Primary School, Billinge

Cow Haiku

Around the farm fields,
The cow moves briskly and slow,
Small horse on the go.

Patrick Lynch (10)
St Mary's Birchley RC Primary School, Billinge

Beyond The Door

(Based on 'The Door' by Miroslav Holub)

Go and open the door.
Maybe outside there's
a secret forest
or a golden paradise,
a stone bird
or a mad magician.

Go and open the door.
Maybe a dinosaur,
maybe a golden castle
or maybe a spooky old cave
or a very old library.

Go and open the door.
If it is only the wind growling
it will still make a draught.

Olivia Tickle (8)
St Mary's Birchley RC Primary School, Billinge

In A Moment Of Silence

In a moment of silence underground,
I heard burrowing badgers digging a hole.

In a moment of silence on the moon,
I heard a shimmering, shooting star sweep across the sky.

I a moment of silence inside an apple,
I heard a wriggling worm.

In a moment of silence on Christmas Eve,
I heard a cracking creak, who could it be?

In a moment of silence at the North Pole,
I heard the whistling wind going through the air.

In a moment of silence inside a computer,
I heard big beeping electronics that would not stop.

Daniel Twist (9)
St Mary's Birchley RC Primary School, Billinge

Inside My Marble

Inside my marble I can see boiling hot lava
surrounded by eight vicious dragons,

Inside my marble I can see me living in a land
of marshmallows and chocolate,

Inside my marble I can see me playing for Liverpool
holding the cup and me being the best player in the world.

Inside my marble I can see my house
made out of sweets,

Inside my marble I can see a red dragon
blowing smoke flames all over an orange dragon,

Inside my marble I can see my house
blowing up,

I would love to live inside my marble.

Nicholas Clark (8)
St Mary's Birchley RC Primary School, Billinge

Dreaming Is Like . . .

Dreaming is like being on another planet,
Dreaming is like meeting the Snow Queen,
Dreaming is like landing on the moon,
Dreaming is like flying in the sky,
Dreaming is like a pool of feathers,
Dreaming is like a boat flying in the air,
Dreaming is like being stuck in the Land of Oz,
Dreaming is like having a 30cm piece of chocolate
All to myself.

Robyn Ashby (8)
St Mary's Birchley RC Primary School, Billinge

Dreaming Is Like . . .

Dreaming is like jumping into a pool of feathers
Dreaming is like being on another planet
Dreaming is like being in a book
Dreaming is like flying in the sky
Dreaming is like being stuck in the land of Christmas
Dreaming is like eating chocolate all day
Dreaming is like winning the lottery
Dreaming is like meeting Frosty the snowman.

Olivia Mahoney (8)
St Mary's Birchley RC Primary School, Billinge

I Want To Paint

I want to paint a silly face
I want to paint a boy eating paste
I want to paint a cat's head
I want to paint me in bed
I want to paint a sleeping dog
I want to paint a jumping frog
I want to paint a simple flower
I want to paint Superman without power.

Lauren Halsall (9)
St Mary's Birchley RC Primary School, Billinge

Lion Haiku

On the jungle floor,
Runs a roaring, hungry lion,
Like a dinosaur.

Melissa French (10)
St Mary's Birchley RC Primary School, Billinge

Snowy Snowball

It moves quick like Concorde
and flashes faster than a blink of an eye
and falls like an angel
falling gracefully from the sky.

It feels soft and gentle
and very slushy and wild
and the children put their hands up.

Will Ainsworth (8)
St Paul's RC Primary School, Feniscowles

A Shimmering Snowflake

It is thin and light, it feels chilly and soft
It feels cold and slippery.
It makes you feel tingly when you touch it
Listen to the silence it makes in the air
Watch the gentle, glittery snowflake fall to the ground
It melts on your tongue and tastes like water.

Eleanor Rawstron (8)
St Paul's RC Primary School, Feniscowles

Clear, Cold Raindrop

Clear, cold, dripping, dashing,
sparkling, racing rain.
It is storming down to the floor.

Poppy Birtwistle (7)
St Paul's RC Primary School, Feniscowles

A Sparkly, Shiny Snowflake

A cold, chilly snowflake falls to the ground
A soft, wet, icy snowflake
It glitters all day and night
It is white and crystal clear
Melts on your tongue
Lovely and bright.

Jenny Parker (7)
St Paul's RC Primary School, Feniscowles

Snowy Snowflake

A silent snowflake slowly falling from the sky
He wants company but he has died
A crystal, light, glittering snowflake
That is tiny and icy, where the children play
I think it makes me chilly and cold.

John Wilcock (7)
St Paul's RC Primary School, Feniscowles

A Rainy Day

The fresh clean raindrops coming down,
The rain comes from the clouds,
The freezing cold rain going down.

Marcus Eccles (7)
St Paul's RC Primary School, Feniscowles

Shiny Sun

The winter sun hides
behind the grey smoky clouds and waits
for the children to play.

Mollie Beattie (8)
St Paul's RC Primary School, Feniscowles

What Is Weather?

Cold, shiny, gushing,
pitter-patter,
racing across the sky.
I fall from the sky in a dash.

Kate Flanagan (7)
St Paul's RC Primary School, Feniscowles

A Raindrop

A raindrop is fast and small,
Clear as a crystal when a light shines on it,
As fresh as a stream in summer
And some rain runs.

Benjamin O'Ryan (8)
St Paul's RC Primary School, Feniscowles

Rushing Rain

Pitter-patter, splash,
The rain is streaming down.
Pitter-patter, pitter-patter,
It's splashing on the floor from the clouds.

Danielle Cottey (8)
St Paul's RC Primary School, Feniscowles

Rushing Down The Sky

The rain is fresh and fast
Streaming down the road.
A drizzly raindrop falling from the cloud.

Rachael Cross (7)
St Paul's RC Primary School, Feniscowles

Rushing Raindrops

I come from the clouds
and crash on the floor, I sometimes go fast,
I sometimes go slow, I drizzle along
and go flow, *splash*.

Adam Steven Burgess (7)
St Paul's RC Primary School, Feniscowles

My Magic Box

(Based on 'Magic Box' by Kit Wright)

I will put in my magic box . . .

Snowflakes falling to the floor,
A flash of lightning through a tree,
A giraffe stretching its neck to reach food.

I will put in my magic box . . .

A glistening unicorn's horn,
The sound of a horse galloping against the wind,
The sun shining through the sky.

I will put in my magic box . . .

A puppy being born,
Seeing the Minotaur roaring in the maze
Staring into Medusa's eyes.

I will put in my magic box . . .

A big, ruby stone gleaming in a shop window,
A horse galloping like a bird in the sky,
The cat's eyes gleaming in the night sky.

Charlotte Wyatt (10)
Sabden Primary School, Clitheroe

My Magic Box

(Based on 'Magic Box' by Kit Wright)

I will put in my magic box . . .

The colours of fireworks in the night sky,
The twinkle of a precious diamond,
The first snowflake of winter.

I will put in my magic box . . .

The warmth of a bonfire on a cold night,
The hoot of an owl at midnight,
The soft wail of a lamb just two days old.

I will put in my magic box . . .

The red breast of a robin singing in the morning,
The smell of cooked breakfast toast on a Sunday.

Jack Heywood (10)
Sabden Primary School, Clitheroe

My Magic Box

(Based on 'Magic Box' by Kit Wright)

I will put in my magic box . . .

The silver of the sparkling stars,
A bit of a dark cave,
The silver of a spider's cobweb.

I will put in my magic box . . .

The soft wool of a newborn lamb,
The wand of the golden fairy,
The smell of the roses' petals.

Leoni Grace Holmes (9)
Sabden Primary School, Clitheroe

My Magic Box

(Based on 'Magic Box' by Kit Wright)

I will put in my magic box . . .

A smooth dolphin swimming in the glistening ocean,
A spider spinning a delicate web,
An owl hooting in the night.

I will put in my magic box . . .

A horse's golden hoof getting worn out,
A unicorn's glittering horn shining all day,
Autumn leaves falling on the golden floor.

I will put in my magic box . . .

A tiny kitten calling for its food,
A stone shimmering all through the day,
The sun rising in the desert.

I will put in my magic box . . .

The coldness of the sea reaching my feet.

Lauren Bywater (10)
Sabden Primary School, Clitheroe

My Magic Box

(Based on 'Magic Box' by Kit Wright)

I will put in my magic box . . .

A sparkling, ruby-red ring from a famous pop star
A unicorn running through the forest,
The glistening shine of a golden swan.

I will put in my magic box . . .

The smell of a chocolate cake baking in the oven,
The sparkle of a firework exploding in the night sky.

Charlotte Knowles (10)
Sabden Primary School, Clitheroe

My Magic Box

(Based on 'Magic Box' by Kit Wright)

I will put in my magic box . . .

A heron catching fish in the river,
Dolphins guiding boats to shore,
Antelope walking slowly on a path.

I will put in my magic box . . .

The world's biggest cat creeping around,
The sea's waves crashing against the cliffs
Foxes' cubs playing around.

I will put in my magic box . . .

A baby calf nuzzling its mum,
A pony's white tail,
Birds twittering in the mist.

Samantha Booth (9)
Sabden Primary School, Clitheroe

My Magic Box

(Based on 'Magic Box' by Kit Wright.)

I will put in my magic box . . .

The sound of a salmon jumping up a misty waterfall,
The feel of excitement on a snowy Christmas morning,
Thick snow at Christmas time.

I will put in my magic box . . .

The spray of the sea on a grey misty morning,
The first firework on Bonfire Night,
The flickering flames on a big bonfire.

James Smith (10)
Sabden Primary School, Clitheroe

My Magic Box

(Based on 'Magic Box' by Kit Wright)

I will put in my magic box . . .

Halley's Comet from outer space,
A bat's eye, golden like brass,
A rhino's horn as long as snakes.

I will put in my magic box . . .

A magic sword glinting like silver,
The pattern of a giraffe like brown poppies,
The beautiful marbling on snow-white paper.

I will put in my magic box . . .

The magical colourful pink and red fading sunsets,
A huge diamond twinkling colours red, blue and purple.

Joe Wickham (9)
Sabden Primary School, Clitheroe

My Magic Box

(Based on 'Magic Box' by Kit Wright)

I will put in my magic box . . .

Freshly fallen snow on Christmas Eve,
The sound of a horse galloping on freshly mown grass,
The quiet bark of a newborn puppy.

I will put in my magic box . . .

The smell of woods on a frosty morning,
The sight of fireworks on Bonfire Night,
The sound of wrapping paper on Christmas Day.

Amy Bond (10)
Sabden Primary School, Clitheroe

My Magic Box

(Based on 'Magic Box' by Kit Wright)

I will put in my magic box . . .

A shimmering star twinkling in the moonlit sky,
The crystal clear waterfall hitting the sharp-edged rocks,
The twinkling gleam of my cat's green eyes.

I will put in my magic box . . .

Clinking coins clattering on the ground,
A silky white pearl glittering on the dress,
The whisper of the autumn leaves falling.

I will put in my magic box . . .

A glittering golden eagle swooping in the air,
The sound of a horse's hooves clattering in the distance,
The gleam of a firework in the midnight sky.

Laura Proctor (11)
Sabden Primary School, Clitheroe

My Magic Box

(Based on 'Magic Box' by Kit Wright)

I will put in my magic box . . .

A magic wand waving in the pitch-black sky,
An endless supply of my favourite sweets,
Father Christmas coming early in the morning.

I will put in my magic box . . .

The biggest firework on Bonfire Night,
A lot of money for me to spend,
A silver Aston Martin car.

Peter Byrne (10)
Sabden Primary School, Clitheroe

My Magic Box

(Based on 'Magic Box' by Kit Wright)

In my magic box I will put . . .

A silver stone from a moonlit beach,
A Christmas snowflake falling through the air,
A butterfly landing on a silken poppy.

In my magic box I will put . . .

A gushing stream on a crisp spring morning,
The crisp air blowing through the autumn trees,
The first star lit at night.

In my magic box I will put . . .

A woodland wind whistling through the forest trees,
The silhouette of a barn owl over the midnight hill,
A kitten's fur, soft and warm.

Naomi Cull (10)
Sabden Primary School, Clitheroe

My Magic Box

(Based on 'Magic Box' by Kit Wright)

I will put in my magic box . . .

A blazing sun in the middle of a burning desert,
A comfy slipper on my foot,
A shining silver boot from my favourite footballer.

I will put in my box . . .

A Roman soldier ready for battle,
A gleaming silver bullet from a soldier sniper,
A red-hot grenade blowing up the Germans.

Ben Scott (10)
Sabden Primary School, Clitheroe

My Magic Box
(Based on 'Magic Box' by Kit Wright)

I will put in my magic box . . .

The glint of Saturn's rings through a telescope,
A gorgeous rearing stallion on a treacherous cliff top,
The eerie silence of a black forest at midnight.

I will put in my magic box . . .

The gentle padding of a dog's paws on the frozen ground,
The whinny of a young filly on a freezing winter's night,
The horrific clatter of silver swords in battle.

I will put in my magic box . . .

The swish of colourful pom-poms at the cheerleading international,
The sapphire night sky dotted with silver stars,
The golden eyes of a fluffy snowy-white owl.

Ashlin Orrell (11)
Sabden Primary School, Clitheroe

My Magic Box
(Based on 'Magic Box' by Kit Wright)

I will put in my magic box . . .

The glisten of the dew on the morning grass,
The horses' hooves padding along the golden beach,
The moon casting a shimmer across the sky.

I will put in my magic box . . .

The howl of a dog in the nearby kennels,
The sun sinking behind the horizon,
The shimmer of a dolphin rising above the waves.

Elizabeth Crossley (10)
Sabden Primary School, Clitheroe

My Magic Box

(Based on 'Magic Box' by Kit Wright)

In my magic box I will put . . .
The flash of lights,
The first snowflake to fall at Christmas.

In my magic box I will put . . .

A golden piece of glittering stone,
A golden hoof of a precious horse,
A golden trophy glinting in the sun.

In my magic box I will put . . .

A silky hair from a unicorn,
A gleaming, shining cat's eye,
A spark of a firework in the lit-up sky.

Mary Gill (11)
Sabden Primary School, Clitheroe

World Cup

(My poem of celebration about England's World Cup triumph)

14 million watched to see
English rugby team making history.

At 9 o'clock the game began,
As I sat there eating toast and jam.

Scrums, tackles and loads of action,
Good job we have Jonny Wilkinson.

Hands together, ready to kick,
Oh yes! 20-17, what a trick.

We've won, we've won, everyone stands up,
England has won the World Cup!

Joannah Riley (9)
Sudell School, Darwen

Rugby World Cup
(My poem of celebration about England's Rugby World Cup triumph)

You know how much it means to me and the football players,
When they start to kick off, I turn over the TV,
When they score a goal, I shout, 'Hip, hip, hooray!'
But when they don't score and the other team scores,
I shout, 'Boo! Boo!'
But I am here today to celebrate the Rugby World Cup
that England's team has won.

Natasha Tomlinson (7)
Sudell School, Darwen

The Rugby World Cup
(My poem of celebration about England's Rugby World Cup triumph)

England won the Rugby World Cup and we're truly very proud,
They made it look so easy and astonished their adoring crowd.
The players entered the pitch to a loud and deafening roar,
The fans just couldn't wait to see their home team score.
It was a thrilling match, we couldn't believe our eyes,
It was so exciting that England won the prize!

Georgina Southern (10)
Sudell School, Darwen

England's Success
(My poem of celebration about England's Rugby World Cup triumph)

England won the test because they are better than all the rest,
England's rose always does a pose when they are winning a match.
Red and white won the fight against Australia and *that's right!*

Siân-Marie Barlow (10)
Sudell School, Darwen

England World Cup

(My poem of celebration about England's Rugby World Cup triumph)

I watched rugby, it was good,
They scored a goal
And made a hole,
They kicked it
And whipped it,
They kicked it so hard
And made it so tough,
The rugby was hot,
And made a good shot.
I jumped for joy because
England won the rugby match.
That was the end of the brilliant game,
It was Sunday when I watched the rugby.

Shannon Groves (7)
Sudell School, Darwen

Rugby World Cup

(My poem of celebration about England's Rugby World Cup triumph)

England need a rest,
Because they always try to do their best,
They work together to score goals,
We work together to achieve our goals.
They never talk back
But sometimes we do!
We try to make our school the best,
And England need to do too.

Briony Bamber (9)
Sudell School, Darwen

It Was In Jonny's Hands

(My poem about England's Rugby World Cup triumph)

Down Under was the venue,
Rugby was the game,
Australia Vs England,
At last the time came
For us to beat the Aussies,
Oh what a wonderful day.

Both teams scored many a try,
30 seconds to go;
It was in Jonny's hands,
The crowd went quiet,
I couldn't look,
But yes, they had done it,
They'd won the World Cup!

Amy Lucas (11)
Sudell School, Darwen

England

(My poem of celebration about England's Rugby World Cup triumph)

E veryone loves them,
N ow they've won the cup,
G old shining brightly,
L ining up to meet the fans,
A good team,
N ow they've won, *yeah!*
D own the road, the crowds cheer.

Siobhan McKenna (10)
Sudell School, Darwen

The England World Cup

(My poem of celebration about England's Rugby World Cup triumph)

England play Australia in a rugby match,
A ball is thrown into the air, someone has to catch,
The men all gather in a rugby scrum,
They concentrate hard but look so glum,
They pass the ball and kick it high,
Look as it goes, it seems to fly
Towards the post, they score a try.
'Hooray, hooray,' the crowds cry.
England have scored, they are the winning nation,
The team return home to a fine celebration.

Sophie Birtwell (8)
Sudell School, Darwen

Rugby World Cup

(My poem of celebration about England's Rugby World Cup triumph)

We shall give praise
with love and grace,
to show we can win,
that's when triumph will begin,
from boys to men
we shall win again,
with love and esteem,
oh, what a great team.

Jodi Lee Williams (8)
Sudell School, Darwen

England Won

(My poem of celebration about England's Rugby World Cup triumph)

England won the rugby match,
The last minute got the catch.

In Australia wherever you go,
England *go, go, go.*

Jonny Wilkinson once again won,
Making rugby extra fun.

Rugby is the best,
Better than the rest.

Say it 'England *won, won, won.'*

Yusra Naweed (8)
Sudell School, Darwen

More We Play Together

(My poem of celebration about England's Rugby World Cup triumph)

The more we play together,
together, together,
the more we play together,
the happier we will be.
'Cause your friends are my friends,
and my friends are your friends.
The more we play together,
the happier we will be.

Tammy Atkin (8)
Sudell School, Darwen

Teamwork
(My poem about England's celebration of England's Rugby World Cup triumph)

T eamwork means we all do the right thing,
E ven if you don't want to,
A nd if one person lets you down, it doesn't work as well,
M ight you have something wrong with you?
W hatever it is, just try and sort it out,
O r if you're worried about something, don't let it get you down,
R ugby, England had to work together to win,
K ick teamwork into your life because teamwork matters.

Laura McPhee (10)
Sudell School, Darwen

Rugby
(My poem of celebration about England's Rugby World Cup triumph)

Rugby players are keen to win the cups from all over the world.
England's rugby players win the cup.
They never fail to bring it home.
They never stop working together as a team,
Like at school we're supposed to.
They tried their best to get the cup
As they practise well enough.

Shauna Flynn (9)
Sudell School, Darwen

England's Rugby
(My poem of celebration about England's Rugby World Cup triumph)

England's rugby won the World Cup,
Thanks to Jonny Wilkinson's foot.

We beat them on their own ground,
That's what makes me proud, because
We're England. I will shout out loud.

Trevina McKenna (10)
Sudell School, Darwen

England Won
(My poem of celebration about England's Rugby World Cup triumph)

England won,
England won
The Rugby World Cup.

We love England,
We love England's rugby,
We watched the match
And they won.
It was fab.

Tanya Turner (8)
Sudell School, Darwen

Well Done England!
(My poem of celebration about England's Rugby World Cup triumph)

The winners are the best,
Made only a test
So they can win.

The cup is so good,
I bet they're in the mood
To have some fun!
Well done England!

Paige Sharpe (8)
Sudell School, Darwen

Rugby Rugby
(My poem of celebration about England's Rugby World Cup triumph)

Rugby, rugby, England is the best,
Rugby, rugby, you played better than the rest.
Rugby, rugby, you have the World Cup,
Rugby, rugby, be proud, we are,
And hold it *up!*

Zachary Grunshaw (9)
Sudell School, Darwen

Happiness

(My poem of celebration about England's Rugby World Cup triumph)

The supporters roar with happiness
As Jonny Wilkinson scores the goal.
A perfect minute of a perfect day,
For coaches, managers and all,
Boozers all get blasted,
Players all get drunk,
For this is a celebration for England's Rugby World Cup.

Kids go wild at parents,
Grandparents laugh with joy,
The day will go down in history,
A day full of triumph and joy.

Chelsea Tattersall (10)
Sudell School, Darwen

World Cup

(My poem of celebration about England's Rugby World Cup triumph)

The rain it poured without lightning and thunder,
That glorious game played Down Under.
Johnson's boys strode proudly onto the pitch,
We hoped it would go without a hitch.
The team in gold put up a brave fight,
But they were no match for our men in white.
In extra time on the edge of my seat,
Waiting for a goal from Jonny's marvellous feet.
Woodward's men are a wonderful team,
They have fulfilled our nation's dream.

Kerryn Yarwood (8)
Sudell School, Darwen

Fantastic

(My poem of celebration about England's Rugby World Cup triumph)

F ans watching anxiously,
A waiting the results,
N ever as much tension
T o watch a rugby game.
A s England takes leadership,
S creams start to fill the air,
T he team working so well together,
I s what's really got to get them going,
C ongratulations England!

Hayley Smith (8)
Sudell School, Darwen

Mum!

Mum!
Your toes are like ten fat sausages
Mum!
Your feet are like two rotten pancakes
Mum!
Your knees are like two big rocks
Mum!
Your legs are like two big drumsticks
Mum!
Your belly is like a bowl of jelly
Mum!
Your fingers are like small flowers
Mum!
Your head is like a football
Mum!
Your hair is like a very pretty hedgehog
Mum!
Your backside is like a big potato.
Mum!

Lucy Copeland (8)
Thorp Primary School, Royton

Mum!

Mum!
Her head is like a rugby ball,
Mum!
Her bushy, curly hair is just like a nits' home,
Mum!
Her beautiful blue eyes are sparkling like stars,
Mum!
Her nostrils are like hairy armpits,
Mum!
Her big, thin, bushy eyebrows are just like mine,
Mum!
Her ears stick up like elves' ears,
Mum!
Her scrawny, skinny big lips are just like Big Momma's,
Mum!
Her arms are marching, swinging soldiers' arms,
Mum!
Her elbows are like knobbly knees,
Mum!
Her belly's like thousands of glasses of beer,
Mum!
Her knees are knobbly like mountain tops,
Mum!
Her feet are like two bananas,
Mum!
Her wriggly toes are like wriggly worms,
Mum!
Her soul is deep down and, of course, kind,
Mum!
Her heart is beating fast with pure love,
Mum!
She's the best mum in the whole universe.
I love my mum.

Naomi Slater (8)
Thorp Primary School, Royton

Grandma!

Your nails are like 20 bouncy balls
Grandma!
Your feet are like 2 rulers
Grandma!
Your legs are like rolled up carpets
Grandma!
Your knees are like blobs of jelly
Grandma!
Your backside is like firm CDs
Grandma!
Your back is like elastic bands
Grandma!
Your chest is like a shield for war
Grandma!
Your throat is like a pencil case
Grandma!
Your arms are like 2 twigs
Grandma!
Your head is like a ball of wool
Grandma!
Your eyes are like stars
Grandma!
Your mouth is like a pencil.

Demi Leigh Walton (8)
Thorp Primary School, Royton

Me!

Me!
My head is like a big, round ball.
Me!
My eyes are like the big, blue sea.
Me!
My ears are like two rabbit's ears.
Me!
My nostril is like a deep, dark cave.
Me!
My mouth is like a ticking clock.
Me!
My hands are like two big books.
Me!
My legs are like two big walking sticks.
Me!
My backside is like a flat pancake.

Ruth Sudlow (9)
Thorp Primary School, Royton

Mum!

Mum!
Your face is as pretty as a flower
Mum!
Your eyes are like two brown, bouncy balls
Mum!
Your mouth is as red as a rose
Mum!
Your tummy is like a bold rock near the sea
Mum!
Your legs are like flower stems
Mum!
Your feet are like the petals on a lily
Mum!
You are the best!

Ellis Hudson (9)
Thorp Primary School, Royton

Me!

Me,
my head is like a football.
Me,
my eyes are like Mars and Earth.
Me,
my ears are like computer screens.
Me,
my nostrils are like ear wax.
Me,
my mouth is like some car wheels.
Me,
my hands are like crocodiles.
Me,
my belly is like candy.
Me,
my legs are like sheds.
Me,
my backside is like a school roof.

Taylor Greenwood (8)
Thorp Primary School, Royton

Auntie Suz!

Auntie Suz!
Your feet are like flat windows
Auntie Suz!
Your legs are like wooden sticks
Auntie Suz!
Your tummy is like a computer
Auntie Suz!
Your mouth is like a cave
Auntie Suz!
Your eyes are like the sea
Auntie Suz!

Catherine Boone (8)
Thorp Primary School, Royton

Dad

Dad!
Your hair is like a mountain top.
Dad!
Your eyes are like bouncy balls.
Dad!
Your mouth is like a mane.
Dad!
Your chest is like the biggest lemon.
Dad!
Your backside is like huge rocks.
Dad!
Your nose is like a motocross ramp.
Dad!
Your legs are like two tree logs.
Dad!
Your feet are like bananas that smell rotten.

Courtney Chappell (9)
Thorp Primary School, Royton

Adam!

Adam!
Your hair is like trees.
Adam!
Your mouth is like whipped cream.
Adam!
Your eyes are like red-hot flames.
Adam!
Your ears are like sunny shaped rocks.
Adam!
Your backside is like 2 footballs.
Adam!
Your legs are like 2 cannons.

Luke Hamilton (9)
Thorp Primary School, Royton

Dad!

Dad!
Dad your head is like a football.

Dad!
Dad your eyes are like grapes.

Dad!
Dad your legs are like walking sticks.

Dad!
Dad your hair is like a black mop.

Dad!
Dad your arms are like two tigers.

Dad!
Dad your mouth is like a circle.

Dad!
Dad your backside's like a mountain.

Daniel Hawthorne (8)
Thorp Primary School, Royton

I Want . . .

I want a car
So I can drive around.

I want some sweets
That I don't have to share.

I want to go on holiday
So I can splash in the pool.

I want a puppy
That I can play with.

I want those girls to play with me
Because they are playing a good game.

Anna Blythe (8)
Walmsley Primary School, Egerton

Dad Won't Let Me

I want to be a skydiver but Dad won't let me,
I want to dig to China but Dad said it was too far.
I want to swim to France but Dad said I will get eaten by a shark.
I want to work in a zoo but Dad said I would get eaten by a tiger.
I want to be a footballer but Dad said I will kick somebody.
'What can I be Dad?'
'My shop assistant!'
'Ah Dad!'

Joshua Povah (10)
Walmsley Primary School, Egerton

Mum Won't Let Me

I want to go in a limo but Mum won't let me,
I want to go bungee jumping but Mum won't let me.
I'd like to go to Rome but Mum won't let me,
I want to go to see Ronaldo but Mum won't let me.
I want to play football every day but Mum won't let me.
I really want to see someone in the army but Mum won't let me.
I want a dog but Mum won't let me.
The only thing I am allowed to do is *homework!*

Charlie Bleasdale (9)
Walmsley Primary School, Egerton

Detention

I'm getting really excited it's nearly the end of school,
I'm going to my friend's house and I'm going to the pool.
Oh school, school why won't it end?
I want to see my friend.
At last the bell begins to ring
And I get to see her.
Oh no, guess what?
Detention!

Anna Hughes (8)
Walmsley Primary School, Egerton

Who Do You Think You Are?

Who do you think you are, putting jelly in my welly?
Who do you think you are, sitting on the telly?

Who do you think you are, jumping on the bed?
Who do you think you are, pulling fluff out of Ted?

Who do you think you are, eating all my snack?
Who do you think you are, ripping up my backpack?

Who do you think you are, stamping on my glasses?
Who do you think you are, tearing up Mum's bus passes?

Who do you think you are, scattering leaves with the rake?
Who do you think you are, breaking my toys for goodness sake?

Who do you think you are, looking in my Man Utd pencil case?
Who do you think you are, messing up my make-up for my face?

Who do you think you are, standing on my castle made out of sand?
Who do you think you are, plucking my violin that I play in a band?

Emma Foudy (9)
Walmsley Primary School, Egerton

I Want . . .

For my birthday I want a Ferrari,
All bright and light and speedy.
For my birthday I want a box of computer games,
So entertaining that I could never get bored with them.
For my birthday I want a bag of chocolate,
So creamy and delicious I would never get bored with the taste.
For my birthday I want a new bike,
With countless gears and gold-plated handlebars.
I would love all these things but the best presents for me
Are the ones you can share with the whole family.

Sam Haslam (9)
Walmsley Primary School, Egerton

Why?

Why is the sky always blue?
Why does he always pick on you?
Why? Why? Why?

Why does the taste of wine make my heart
feel like sunshine?
Oh why? Oh why? Oh why?

Why do dogs shake when they're all wet?
I get bitten by my next-door neighbour's pet snake.
Why?

Never mind all those who are unkind,
I don't care what they find!
Because that's how God made them.

Jack Williams (10)
Walmsley Primary School, Egerton

I Want To Be . . .

I want to be an astronaut floating in the sky,
I want to be a footballer on the field.
I want to be a diver in the sea,
I want to be a limo driver, driving people around.
I want to be a chef in a fancy restaurant,
I want to be an entertainer at a funfair.
I want to be an author, writing books all day,
I want to be a pop star singing to crowds of people.
I want to be in the army, fighting Saddam Hussein.

These are the things I want to be!

Andrew Seal (8)
Walmsley Primary School, Egerton

The Big Old Oak Tree

As I stand underneath the big old oak tree
I see many coloured leaves catching the breeze
and fluttering down to the soft green grass below.
As I stand underneath the big old oak tree
I watch flocks of birds catching the wind and soaring off
to warmer lands for the winter.
As I stand underneath the big old oak tree
I see a field of crops in the distance, as golden as the
blazing sun in summertime.
As I stand underneath the big old oak tree
I watch fat, puffy clouds sailing slowly over the
darkening, grey sky.
As I stand underneath the big old oak tree
I watch the squirrels scurrying down the tree trunks,
collecting nuts and berries for the long, cruel winter nights ahead.
As I stand underneath the big old oak tree
I think about the hardships winter brings for everyone
and how lucky we are,
As I stand underneath the big old oak tree.

Cameron Smith (9)
Walmsley Primary School, Egerton

I Would Like To Paint

I would like to paint the feel of fresh grass
I would like to paint the taste of chocolate
I would like to paint the feel of the wind
I would like to paint the taste of an apple
I would like to paint the feel of the brushes
I would like to paint the taste of fresh bread
I would like to paint the feel of the clouds.

Ben Rouse (9)
Walmsley Primary School, Egerton

In A Moment Of Silence

In a moment of silence I heard
a war breaking out.

In a moment of silence I heard
the shot of a gun.

In a moment of silence I heard
the destructive bang of a bomb.
Bang!

In a moment of silence I heard
a ground missile being fired.

In a moment of silence I heard
a German tank blow up.

In a moment of silence I heard
this poem conclude!

Jordan McDermott (8)
Walmsley Primary School, Egerton

But My Mum Said 'No!'

I want my friends to come to my house to sleep,
But my mum said, 'No!'

I want to have another dog,
But my mum said, 'No!'

I want my own bedroom
But my mum said, 'No!'

I want to go to Disneyland
But my mum said, 'No!'

I hope soon my mum will say 'Yes!'

Olivia O'Dowd (8)
Walmsley Primary School, Egerton

In A Moment Of Silence

In a moment of silence I heard
a caterpillar eating a leaf,

In a moment of silence I heard
a dog wagging its tail.

In a moment of silence I heard
a dog scratching its ear.

In a moment of silence I heard
a fish swimming in a pond.

In a moment of silence I heard
a bird singing a song.

In a moment of silence I heard
a horse pulling up grass.

In a moment of silence I heard
a squirrel eating a nut.

In a moment of silence I heard
the bees making honey.

Megan Latham (10)
Walmsley Primary School, Egerton

I Want To, But Mum Won't Let Me

I want to go to the moon but Mum won't let me,
I want to join the army but Mum won't let me.
I want to be a policeman but Mum won't let me,
I want to skip school but Mum won't let me.
I want to go to my friend's house but Mum won't let me.
I want to get a cat but Mum won't let me,
I want to get a PlayStation but Mum won't let me.
She just won't let me do anything.
'What can I do then Mum?'

Michael Watkin (8)
Walmsley Primary School, Egerton

But My Mum Won't Let Me

I want my friends to come to my house,
But my mum won't let me.

I want to play the piano,
But my mum won't let me.

I want to have a dog,
But my mum won't let me.

I want to go to Lapland
But my mum won't let me.

I wish I could do all of these things
And my mum that would say 'Yes!'

Abbie Leatham (8)
Walmsley Primary School, Egerton

Mum Won't Let Me

I want to be a mermaid, splashing in the sea
but Mum won't let me.

I want to be a pop star, singing away
but Mum won't let me

I want to be a ballerina, dancing on my toes
but Mum won't let me

I want to go trampolining, bouncing on my feet
but Mum won't let me.

'Mum, what can I do?'

Beth Johnson (9)
Walmsley Primary School, Egerton

Who Do You Think You Are?

Who do you think you are, putting jelly in my welly?
Who do you think you are, swearing at Ellie?

Who do you think you are, climbing the Eiffel Tower?
Who do you think you are, putting in my cake, a bag of flour?

Who do you think you are, eating all the food?
Who do you think you are, thinking you're a cool dude?

Who do you think you are, whacking Tracy on the head?
Who do you think you are, bouncing on the bed?

Who do you think you are, being nasty to all my friends?
Who do you think you are, driving Mum's Mercedes Benz?

Who do you think you are, ripping up my Mickey Mouse?
Who do you think you are, running round the house?

Who do you think you are messing up my room?
Who do you think you are putting a mummy in a cardboard box tomb?

Charlotte Edwards (9)
Walmsley Primary School, Egerton

Earthquakes

An earthquake's struck!
Shake, rumble, crash!
The shivering of plates underground
Make the people around that place
Scream till their voices are out
After it's struck -
There's big cracks in the land
The people stare at the remains
Everyone will look back at the day when
The earthquake struck!

Michael Kelly (8)
Walmsley Primary School, Egerton

Decorating The Christmas Tree

I'll decorate the Christmas tree
With fairies and pretty lights,
I'll decorate the Christmas tree
with tinsel and Turkish delights.

I'll decorate the Christmas tree
With archangels galore,
I'll go to the shop on Monday
and guess what? I'll buy some more!

I'll decorate the Christmas tree
with dangling decorations,
I'll decorate the Christmas tree
and prepare for the celebrations!

I hope you have a nice Christmas
and decorate your tree too.
So send some tips on decorating
and I'll decorate just like you!

Abby Lamb (9)
Walmsley Primary School, Egerton

Colours

Pink is the colour of the sunset down,
Gold is the colour of the Queen's crown.
Black is the colour of the dark pretty night,
Blue is the colour of the sky when it's bright.
Brown is the colour of the useful wood.
White is the colour of the daisy when it's in bud,
Green is the colour of the leaves on a tree,
Peach is the colour of the skin on me.
Orange is the colour of the autumn leaves.
Silver is the colour of my mum's keys.

Hannah Makin (9)
Walmsley Primary School, Egerton

Who Do You Think You Are?

Who do you think you are,
crashing the school computer?

Who do you think you are
sticking bubblegum in my hair?

Who do you think you are
putting jelly in my welly?

Who do you think you are
telling the head teacher off?

Who do you think you are
throwing my cat in the mud?

Who do you think you are?

Millie Hinchliffe (9)
Walmsley Primary School, Egerton

I Wanted

I wanted to climb the Eiffel Tower
but Gran wouldn't let me!

I wanted to dig for treasure
but Gran wouldn't let me!

I wanted to buy a brand new car
but Gran wouldn't let me!

I wanted to go to France
but Gran wouldn't let me!

Oh Gran, if I can't do those things
what can I do?

Lucy Maycox (10)
Walmsley Primary School, Egerton

Snow Is Great

Snow is great, snow is grand
but how do you make a snowman's hand?

Snow falls to the ground just like a feather
but still doesn't make a sound, whatever
the weather.

You have to wear gloves and a hat
to keep you warm and that is that.

Throw snowballs at your mum and dad
and think of all the fun you've had.

Zoom down the hill on your sledge
then take a walk to the river's edge.

Then take a skate on the ice and go home
and have a Christmas bun, that's nice!

Lucy Shaw (9)
Walmsley Primary School, Egerton

What Is . . . ?

What is red?
Red is the sun
Blazing upon the city.

What is yellow?
Yellow is a daffodil
Growing out of the bright
Green grass.

What is pink?
Pink is the sunset
Watching the sun go down.

What is blue?
Blue is the sea
Splashing up into the air.

What is white?
White is the snow
That gets stamped on by everybody.

Katie Brockley (9)
Walmsley Primary School, Egerton

Why? Why? Why?

Why? Why? Why?
Why use bricks to make a wall?
Why? Why? Why?
Why are trees always so tall?
Why? Why? Why?
Why are whiteboards white?
Why? Why? Why?
Why do dogs always bite?
Why? Why? Why?
Why is Emma always late?
Why? Why? Why?
Why does my next-door neighbour have a big gate?
Why? Why? Why?
Why . . . ? Why . . . ? Why?

Christopher Cox (9)
Walmsley Primary School, Egerton

But Mum Won't Let Me

I want to fight a war but Mum won't let me,
I want to climb Mount Everest but Mum won't let me.
I want to go to the moon but Mum won't let me,
I want to meet a gorilla but Mum won't let me.
I want to build a robot but Mum won't let me,
I want to get a mobile phone but Mum won't let me.
I want to play the guitar but Mum won't let me,
I want to play at the Reebok but Mum won't let me.
I want to play for the West Indian cricket team but Mum won't let me,
I want to be a computer expert but Mum won't let me,
I want to be myself and Mum agrees.

Benjamin Finch (9)
Walmsley Primary School, Egerton